...A POETRY CRITICISM READER...

...A POETRY CRITICISM READER...

edited by Jerry Harp
& Jan Weissmiller

UNIVERSITY OF IOWA PRESS...IOWA CITY

University of Iowa Press, Iowa City 52242
Copyright © 2006 by the University of Iowa Press
http://www.uiowa.edu/uiowapress
All rights reserved
Printed in the United States of America
Design by Sara T. Sauers

The University of Iowa Press is a
member of Green Press Initiative and is
committed to preserving natural resources.

Printed on acid-free paper

Cataloging-in-Publication data
on file at the Library of Congress.

06 07 08 09 10 P 5 4 3 2 1

...CONTENTS...

...A POETRY CRITICISM READER...

Introduction
Poetry Criticism after Eliot

...JERRY HARP...

T. S. Eliot was the last figure in English-language poetry who could make ex cathedra statements that commanded attention; whether one agreed or dissented, he was difficult to ignore. As David Perkins puts it in the second volume of his massive *A History of Modern Poetry*, "For twenty-five years T. S. Eliot exercised an authority in the literary world not possessed by any writer before him for more than a century."[1] Or as Seamus Heaney puts the matter, recalling the growth of his own knowledge and sensibility, "one did not need to know any literary thing in particular in the 1950s in order to know that Eliot was the way, the truth and the light, and that until one had found him one had not entered the kingdom of poetry."[2] Surely no one has occupied such a position since, and no doubt many of us find our current moment better suited to pluralist ideals than a literary czarship would likely allow. While Eliot's authority might have kept the high modernist machinery up and running through many of its best years of experimentation, ours is a moment that favors conspicuously multiple, shifting, sometimes overlapping, often competing centers of authority. It may be that something like the current situation is precisely what is called for even these fifty years after the ascendancy of a powerful central figure—a situation of robust fragmentation calling for multiple modes of experiment and exploration.

Nevertheless, we may yet find some basis for our current pluralism in Eliot's thought about tradition, however oblique our gaze must be. In his essay "Tradition and the Individual Talent" (1919), Eliot famously asserts the necessity of a poet constructing a personal tradition composed of the voices from the past that are to exert a formative pressure on the poet's own work. In Eliot's version of the life of poetry, engaging with such a personally constructed tradition is one of the conditions of a poet's strength. Further, such a tradition "cannot be inherited, and if you want it you must obtain it by great labour."[3] Of course, the usual narrative of literary history also points out that in Eliot's era a great portion of the labor of inheritance, especially that of choosing what one is to be influenced by, was carried out by institutions of higher learning with relatively stable notions of literary tradition. No doubt, this version of the narrative is in some ways valid. For evidence of what formed Eliot's idea of tradition, one might begin by looking at Eliot's curriculum of study as a Harvard undergraduate, one that included literary studies in Greek, English, and French along with courses in medieval history and ancient and modern philosophy.[4]

Further clues to Eliot's notion of tradition may be gleaned from his notes to *The Waste Land* (1922) and his essay "What Is a Classic?" (1944).[5] The short answer to the question posed by the essay's title is Virgil's *Aeneid*, a work that answers to the term "classic" in Eliot's relatively narrow use of the word on this occasion, because the *Aeneid* speaks as "the consciousness of Rome and the supreme voice of her language."[6] This language, Latin, is the one that remained for Eliot the supreme and generative inheritance of all European civilization, and for the Eliot of 1919, when he published "Tradition and the Individual Talent," European civilization occupied the position of central concern, for it is "the whole of the literature of Europe"[7] that remains the source of tradition for a poet writing in English. However, adverting to the notes of *The Waste Land*, which include references to the Buddha's Fire Sermon and the *Upanishads*, one can see that as early as 1922 Eliot is bringing at least a smattering of Asian writing and thought into his work. By opening his poem to these latter works, Eliot allows them to exert an influence on his writing and thus to become part of his personally constructed tradition. The very idea of what constitutes tradition remains on the move.

But it seems that Eliot could hardly avoid a dynamic notion not only of tradition but also of the source, or sources, of tradition. One reason for this unsettled notion is that the educational curriculum of Eliot's day was not quite so stable as one might be tempted to think. Gerald Graff has mapped out some of the controversy that marked the early decades of twentieth-century higher education, which inherited from the nineteenth century conflicts between the goals of highly specialized scholarship and the ideals of broadly humanistic education. For partisans of the latter position, laments over the loss of a common culture almost constituted a literary subgenre. As William T. Foster wrote in 1911, "even the general prescription of English is an agreement in name only; what actually goes on under this name is so diverse as to show that we have not yet discerned an 'essential' course in English."[8] Thus, it appears that the ideal of a common culture was unraveling even before one of its guarantors, the "'essential' course in English," could achieve even provisional coherence. That Harvard undergraduates were permitted to choose their own courses was a circumstance that drew the young Eliot's criticism.[9] "Tradition and the Individual Talent" may be read as one young, learned mandarin's response to a situation of perceived crisis.

But we do well to bear in mind the complexity of Eliot's thinking. If he perceived a crisis, he also perceived opportunities in the crisis. In "Tradition and the Individual Talent" he takes the opportunity to articulate a stance in favor of tradition in flexible terms. Even when, two and a half decades later in "What Is a Classic?" he holds up a single work as attaining singularly classic status, he goes on to speak of the advantages of pluralism and diversity. He points out that a given literature's classic period is not necessarily its greatest. On the one hand, he affirms the importance of keeping in our awareness the classic ideal—its maturity of language, mind, and manners, along with its amplitude, comprehensiveness, and perfection of a harmonious and common style; the true classic, he says, is one that manifests the language's genius at a given moment. On the other hand, he opines "that those literatures . . . in which the classical qualities are scattered between various authors and several periods, may well be the richer."[10] In other words, it may be to a literature's advantage to mix, and even dilute, its classic qualities with a diversity of other styles. It is not that Eliot foresaw the pluralism to come but rather that his complex vision, as manifested in both his poetry and his prose, has functioned to help bring about our pluralist age and sensibilities.

If Eliot's notion of tradition was inherently dynamic, then it may be that our sense of tradition at the present moment is appropriately even more expansive and flexible. The term "tradition" (from Latin *tradere*, to hand over, give up, surrender) has roots in ancient Roman law and refers to the usual means whereby ownership of property was transferred or given over.[11] The etymology is informative in that it implies the necessity of taking up and making use of what is handed over if the inheritance is to remain a viable part of culture. In other words, the old property must be integrated into the contemporary lifeworld. The inheritance of riches works as a benefit only if the inheritor makes good use of what the dead have left behind. Part of what our age has become sensitive to are the riches of multiple sources of inheritance.

No doubt our age also does well to bear in mind the sheer labor required to make good use of our literary inheritances—good use that issues in the creation of new voices. As Sir Sidney no doubt knew, despite the conclusion of the first sonnet of *Astrophil and Stella*, it is not enough simply to look in one's heart and write. One reason that such a mode of composition remains inadequate is that much of what is most readily apparent and legible in the heart has been inscribed there by cultural forces. Looking into one's heart to write may be the best way to sound like the blandest version of most everyone else. One of the striking paradoxes of writing is that to achieve one's own distinct voice, one must internalize many other strong voices.[12] It is only by engaging with other voices that one is able to achieve a voice of one's own. But this struggle of engaging with other voices is not the work of the poet only; rather, it is also the work of any strong or considerable critic. Without a thorough knowledge of the literature and critical stances of the past, one's understanding of the present moment's endeavors is bound to ring hollow. At the same time, without some familiarity with the critical and literary stances of the present moment, one's knowledge of the past stands in danger of morbidity. Like the work of the poet, the work of the critic demands the construction of a personal tradition, which is obtained by great labor.

Again, Eliot anticipates these concerns. In "The Function of Criticism" (1923), he begins by quoting a passage from "Tradition and the Individual Talent" to the effect that the whole of a given literature forms an order that is altered in its relationships when something truly new is introduced. He then goes on to assert that "the function of criticism seems to be essentially a problem of order too."[13] The new work of criticism not only comments on literature and literary activity but also carries out its own functions of altering the existing relations among varieties of texts.

In a variety of ways, the pieces included in *A Poetry Criticism Reader* carry out their acts of understanding and enact their judgments in ways that answer to Eliot's ideas about tradition. These essays emphasize ways that poets find new directions by carrying out the difficult labor of creating a tradition from the poetry of the past. Further, the essayists make their own distinct uses of their literary-critical inheritances as they confront the poetry of the present moment. At the same time, a conspicuous presence in many of these essays, along with the poetry that they consider, is popular culture, which sometimes weighs in alongside the more distinctively literary influences. To point this out may be nothing more than to say that many of these pieces, along with the poems they discuss, are distinctively "postmodern," a term that comes up in several of these essays and that calls for some explanation. One way of suggesting the term's range of meanings is to set it alongside the "modernism" that "postmodernism" follows. The poets of the high modernist mode—such as T. S. Eliot, Ezra Pound, Wallace Stevens, and Marianne Moore—came onto the cultural scene at a moment of general perception that the old myths, narratives, and monuments were no longer holding together. While there were yet riches from the glory days of Greece and Rome, from the Jewish and Christian traditions, from the strides of Enlightenment thought, these multiple weaves of culture and their attendant narratives were no longer holding together, nor was any single strand maintaining enough tensile strength to hold together the culture at large. In fact, according to this narrative of the modernist era, the old myths and monuments that had enabled so much of our literature were in fragments.

Hart Crane, who was born about a generation later than these modernist poets, captures well the sense of crisis in his "General Aims and Theories," in which he describes "a world that is so in transition from a decayed culture toward a reorganization of human evaluations that there are few common terms, general denominators of speech that are solid enough or that ring with any vibration or spiritual conviction."[14] The high modernist mode was not trying to reconstruct the old monuments but rather attempting to build something grand and new and monumental out of the old fragments and ruins. Perhaps the most conspicuous examples of this mode of poetic composition remain Eliot's *The Waste Land* and Pound's *Cantos*, works that receive frequent mention in *A Poetry Criticism Reader*.

In contrast to the high modernists, poets of the postmodern mode are pleased to make use of the fragments left over from past moments while at the same time allowing them to remain fragments. In other words, postmodernists sing among the ruins of the past, incorporating these ruins into their performance without attempting to form them into something coherently monumental. In fact, part of what postmodern writers tend to find enabling is the very fragmentariness of the ruins. Fragments make for more portable property to incorporate into one's world. Postmodern modes of writing can both honor the monuments of the past and break down divisions between high and popular culture. They easily combine high seriousness with slapstick humor. They take as much pleasure in withholding as in disclosing. They tend to speak in various voices with a conviction that human identity is multiple and shifting. Postmodern modes tend to engage in writing as a process coming to closures that are always provisional. Postmodernism includes an embrace of disorder without aching after familiar reductions to order. It involves the fragmentation of narratives, not only the grand narratives that hold together great sweeps of history but also the brief and local narratives that make anecdotes familiar.[15]

The foregoing description of postmodernist writing and thought—more suggestive than exhaustive—may prove useful in considering the work of such poets as Jorie Graham, Lyn Hejinian, Paul Muldoon, James Tate, and those whom Stephen Burt styles elliptical poets. At the same time, it is no doubt helpful also to think of these poets as part of the larger trajectory of writers that includes the modernists of the early twentieth century, along with writers of the more remote past. The poets included here continue, after all, to respond to strong poets of the past by seeking to make the language new, to do something with words that has not been done before.

Other poets considered in *A Poetry Criticism Reader*—notably Czeslaw Milosz, Donald Justice, and Seamus Heaney—bear a closer relationship than their younger counterparts to modes of writing which have now clearly become an established part of tradition. Thus, Helen Vendler begins her considerations of Milosz's *A Treatise on Poetry* by setting it alongside Eliot's *The Waste Land*. But then Stephen Yenser uses this latter poem, along with Pound's *Cantos*, to help illuminate Jorie Graham's *Swarm*. And where might one place the poetry of Donald Justice, work that is in many ways allied to that of the high modernists, especially Eliot and Stevens, even as the sensibility appeals very much to the present moment? It is quite apt that Dana Gioia has described Justice as a "postmodern classicist."[16] While the distinctions that separate poets into schools and modes have their uses, it is also important to remain attentive to the blurriness of many boundaries.

Because of the variety of perspectives represented in these pages, it would be difficult to sum up the work of *A Poetry Criticism Reader*—both the work of the critics and that of the poets whom the critics consider—under a single heading. Nor are the poets and critical perspectives represented here meant to exhaust the possibilities. To put the matter quite simply: these are essays that the editors feel represent some of the better and more illuminating poetry criticism in English of the last decade. We have favored essays and reviews that enact their judgments in the midst of thorough attempts to understand and situate historically the poetry under discussion. So far as we know, none of the pieces included here was written in direct response to any of the others; nevertheless, it is our hope that they will complement each other, thus forming a kind of dialogue. Because the editing of *A Poetry Criticism Reader* has been a collaborative effort, its shape differs from what it would have been as the product of either editor working alone. One of the powerful lessons of postmodern thought is that the myth of the ingenious author working in isolation is one that, for our present moment, falsifies more than it illuminates or enables. Writing is a social act that involves dialogue and multiple influences. Dialogue is as much a part of the process of editing as it is of composing poetry and writing criticism.

•••

Many of the pieces that we have chosen were written by poet-critics, and some of these pieces were written by poets as explorations of poetics. One example of this latter kind of essay is Donald Justice's "Of the Music of Poetry" (1997), whose title echoes Eliot's "The Music of Poetry" (1942). In his essay Justice analyzes the old literary-critical trope that links poetry with music, a trope about which Justice's attitude is rather complex. As Justice points out, one encounters musicality in lines that, for example, include a density of such devices as rhyme and alliteration at "the exact point at which plain sense slips momentarily out of reach." Of course, the validation of such sound effects requires "assumptions about the general nature of poetry or else, culturally if not esthetically, a sort of aura about the poet or poem." Justice further notes that one of the assumptions that tends to be linked with the trope of poetry's music is the notion of poetry's imitative sound effects, the idea that the sheer sound of a given passage, apart from the meanings of the words involved, can imitate, for example, softness or anger or comfort. By contrast to this notion of imitation, Justice holds out for the effects of poetry as something in excess of meaning, something constituting a "grace-note of nonsense." Such meanings as arise in a given passage of poetry have much more to do with the denotations of the words than with any supposedly mimetic effects. None of this is to say that there is no such thing, at least in some poems, as a marvelous aptness between meaning and sound, an aptness that many devoted readers have no doubt felt, but rather that this marvelous congruence of meaning and sound cannot be accounted for adequately by a theory of imitation. Finally, Justice maintains that one must acknowledge the very idea of poetry's music as a "metaphor struck off in the heat of wishful thought."

Of the three poetic explorations in this volume, two were written specifically as aesthetic statements. While Jorie Graham affirms in "At the Border" (2002) that theoretical programs have their place at the current moment, she holds out for the importance of temperament in the writing of poetry. What Graham understands her temperament to be leading her poetry toward is experience of "subjectivity and objectivity at their most frayed and fruitful and morally freighted juncture." The poetry resulting from such experience is ideally a call to character, a good-faith vulnerability allowing one, in the midst of the involutions and recursions of one's consciousness, to be seized by moments of surprise in the world. It is a poetry that speaks in a voice of earnestness in the midst of multiple sophistications. It is responsive to and formed more by paradox than by irony. This is a poetry alive to the fluid boundary between subject and object, a poetry formed by deep faith in language's strength balanced by moments when "the human speaker has reached the point where the action of mind takes place in silence." This aesthetic ideal is one open to the many ways that poetry hauls into words what has hitherto remained outside the reach of language.

In "Some Notes toward a Poetics" (2000), Lyn Hejinian articulates an aesthetic position in a philosophical language that engages with such figures as Martin Heidegger and Hannah Arendt. Like Graham, Hejinian affirms a poetry that dwells in uncertainties. The complexity of Hejinian's stance shows in her claim of a poetics of both affirmation and uncertainty, a poetics of "doubt, difficulty, and strangeness." She emphasizes that moments of encounter in human experience happen with the concurrence of coexistence and strangeness, moments when the strange and unfamiliar draw near and cross into the realm of the otherwise familiar. It is in such moments of contact that aesthetic, ethical, and political discovery occurs. The place of such contact, the polis or space of "the sharing of words and deeds," in Hannah Arendt's words,[17] is where one also encounters reality, which is not to be distinguished from appearance. After all, reality or being is that which appears to others as well as to oneself. Since every encounter has about it something of the strange or other, we enter each experience in part as strangers ourselves. Because of the challenges presented by encounters with strangeness, it is easy to approach such moments with the language of comparison, the crossing over of one realm of discourse to another, the dynamics of metaphor. But because these dynamics tend to relate the strange to the familiar, they can deny the emergence of something new by covering over the differences of the other. At the same time, one cannot adequately encounter strangeness without the use of language. In the words of Heidegger, it is language that "lets people and things be there for us." It is the work of poetry to provoke a sense of newness, a sense of the revitalization of the human lifeworld. This work is not, however, that of privileging experience or sensation over intellection. For Hejinian, the experience of sensation, as well as the experience of experience, always occurs enfolded in history and theory.

As mentioned above, several of the essays in *A Poetry Criticism Reader* relate to the term "postmodernism," with its array of meanings. Some of the term's meanings come together in what Stephen Burt calls "The Elliptical Poets" (1998), a term that he coined to describe the work of such contemporary figures as Liam Rector, Mark Levine, Lucie Brock-Broido, Susan Wheeler, and C. D. Wright, among others. These are poets whose work tends to hint at a backstory that is never fully disclosed, thus giving rise to a fragmentation of narrative. The personae of ellipticist poems are provisional and sometimes multiple. The poems tend toward disjunction and confrontation. As Burt puts it, "Ellipticists seek the authority of the rebellious; they want to challenge their readers, violate decorum, surprise or explode assumptions about what belongs in a poem, or what matters in life, and to do so while meeting traditional lyric goals." These are poets whose complicated relationships to literary history leave plenty of room for parody, as there is plenty of room in their poems for shifts from high to popular culture and back again. While these shifts occur, the poems also tend to call into question the very distinction between high and popular culture. The contemporary poet under whose influence the ellipticists labor is clearly Jorie Graham, though they do not try to imitate her. In the postscript, written in 2004 for this anthology, Burt indicates that he wrote "The Elliptical Poets" with the aim of pointing out "an emerging set of styles" rather than a set of hard-and-fast rules or characteristics. He maintains the possibility that ellipticism may in time come to be a kind of mannerism or set of moves that young writers might try out in a stage of their development before moving on.

Another American poet whose work has certain affinities with that of the ellipticists is James Tate. In his "Clarity instead of Order" (1998), James Harms investigates ways in which Tate's poems exist between surrealism and allegory without falling fully into either mode. In Harms's terms, this flirtation with both surrealism and allegory creates many of the specific ways in which Tate's work is postmodern. Tate is a poet of the postmodern moment in a way that involves "an embrace of uncertainty and a valorization of play" in a world of inescapable irony and disorder. By way of contrast to the modernist attempt to master disorder, Tate's postmodernist mode embraces disorder as a condition of its creation. Part of Tate's method is to decontextualize traditional narrative structures, "those grand and organizing principles that are usually there, if only between the lines," and thus to create tales oddly ambiguous in meaning and ambivalent in tone. The voice of a Tate poem tends to be a refraction of identities rather than a unified whole. Tate's poems partake of an almost constant slippage in which a given metaphor's tenor and vehicle (in I. A. Richards's terms) cross and become confused. However, the complexity and confusion of these poems do not exist for their own sake; as Harms's title emphasizes, Tate's poetry seeks lucidity about the chaos that it embraces.

In his review of Paul Muldoon's Hay (1999), Joshua Weiner discusses some of the ways in which Muldoon also is a poet of postmodernity. In Weiner's description the associative and disparate poems of Hay include "diction from different worlds of experience, books, movies, music, cities, mythologies, high and popular culture"; this is work within which one can also discern "fragments of a prior poetry." Muldoon's dense and kaleidoscopic poems are also postmodern in the sense that "Muldoon self-consciously rejects the heroic struggle of building a monument." Muldoon's postmodern improvisations often have him skirting the brink of meaning without crossing over into full disclosure. This is an open-ended poetry energized by the literary past as it faces and moves into the future.

Such also is the poetry of Jorie Graham, as Stephen Yenser emphasizes in his review of *Swarm* (2000). Yenser places Graham's book in a tradition of long poems that includes T. S. Eliot's *The Waste Land*, Ezra Pound's *Cantos*, and David Jones's *Anathemata*. Adverting to the jacket copy's definition of the verb "swarm" as to leave behind a locus of stability "in an attempt, by coming apart, to found a new form that will hold," along with Graham's epigrams from St. Augustine in this volume as well as in her *Region of Unlikeness* (1991), Yenser notes that Graham's poetry is metaphysical in its energies. Further, Yenser takes as a keynote to Graham's writing the "Augustinian motivation to confront candidly whatever the case may be." In its confrontations and its swarming, this is a poetry of spiritual agon, one whose great precursor is the poetry of Emily Dickinson. The terms of the struggle are this: while the divine is in some sense encountered or revealed in the midst of narrative, Graham's narratives remain, like many of her sentences, fragmented. In fact, as Yenser points out, the book as a whole may be better understood as enacting a process—something unpredictable and on the move—than as presenting itself as a mere collection or sequence. The book does not so much conclude as pause "with an emblem sonorously, sensuously saturated with inception." Thus, even as the book draws to a close, it is beginning again.

Several of the pieces in *A Poetry Criticism Reader* are extended considerations of deeply established figures: Donald Justice, Seamus Heaney, and Czeslaw Milosz. In his "In Memory of Orpheus: Three Elegies by Donald Justice" (1998), Mark Jarman takes up Justice's devotion to the arts of both music and poetry. Although best known as a poet, Justice studied musical composition as an undergraduate, under Carl Ruggles at the Univeristy of Miami, and later in his life Justice returned to the composition of musical pieces, several of which were publicly performed. Jarman notes the powerful blending of nostalgia with an elegiac mood in Justice's poems, and he argues that certain of the poems work as movingly as they do because of their relation, whether overt or implied, to the Orpheus myth, "the story of an artist's excellence and loss." In Jarman's estimation, the Orphean journeys of these later poems connect to "some value present but secret in life," a secret value that Jarman conjectures to be related to art, especially the arts of music and poetry.

"'A Lament in Three Voices'" (2001), Helen Vendler's review of Czeslaw Milosz's *A Treatise on Poetry* (2001) and Milosz's *ABC's* (2001), works in part as a summing up of the poet's distinguished career. Vendler favorably compares Milosz's *A Treatise on Poetry* to T. S. Eliot's *The Waste Land*, praising Milosz's poem for its power to burst "the bounds in which it was written." This book-length poem explores the world of Poland before the Second World War and then in its third section "erupts" as "a new barbaric primitivism erases all of culture—art, law, literature, architecture." In the course of her essay, Vendler registers the modulations of texture and tone that characterize the poem as it confronts the Spirit of History on the move, "whistling appetitively at the new post-diluvian opportunities for cultural revolution." But as she goes on to emphasize, Milosz's poetry is also made up of the "language of the senses, the muscles, the fingertips, the body that is at once corporeal and virtual." The fourth section of the *Treatise* has Milosz in the United States seeking solace in nature but coming to the realization that he is and must remain a poet of history rather than of nature; Clio is his muse, not the spirit of the lake. This is the poet, the poet of history, whom we encounter in *Milosz's ABC's*, a collection of prose pieces that Vendler describes as Milosz's "journal of memories." Vendler finds the writing in this journal to be "entertaining, if sometimes intemperate," though she points out that such a formulation cannot sum up the full range of the book's subject matter and tone. This is after all a collection of complex philosophical and theological reflections, as well as personal reminiscences and elegies that do not lose their analytical edge.

Integration, such as that between intellect and instinct, is the keynote of "*Lux Perpetua*" (2002), Dennis O'Driscoll's review of Seamus Heaney's *Electric Light* (2001). In fact, it may be this integration, along with the resulting artistic integrity, that creates the "continuous light" of O'Driscoll's title. O'Driscoll emphasizes that the poems in this collection show an increasing density of classical, biblical, and other literary allusion without losing touch with the instinctual life that, as has often been noted, courses through Heaney's poems. In the book's translations, many of them from

Virgil, Heaney integrates fidelity to the literature from which he translates with responsiveness to the demands of a recognizably contemporary English language. In the elegies of the book's second section, Heaney integrates his uses of various literary voices with his tributes to the dead. At the end of the essay, O'Driscoll takes up the issue with which he began, Blake Morrison's observation that a given volume of Heaney's poetry begins where the previous volume left off. O'Driscoll concludes with his own observations about the complex ways that *Electric Light* connects with Heaney's earlier work as the poet continues—to appropriate the poet's own words—"Steady under strain and strong through tension."

One valuable, and perhaps undervalued, kind of literary endeavor is the recovery of a neglected writer's work. Such is the work that Jenny Penberthy has carried out in her edition of Lorine Niedecker's *Collected Works* (2002). Karen Volkman's review, "Green, Prickly Humanity: Rural Wisconsin's Exhilarating Lost Poet" (2003), emphasizes the sheer variety of Niedecker's poems, prose pieces, and radio plays. If Niedecker is a minimalist, as she has sometimes been labeled, she is an expansive minimalist. Because of Niedecker's relative isolation in "the Wisconsin marshland of Black Hawk Island," she is inevitably compared to Emily Dickinson, as Volkman points out, though Volkman also emphasizes the differences between the two poets. As one moves through the various sections of the *Collected Works*, the poems of Niedecker's *New Goose*, "initially imagined as an updating of Mother Goose reflecting contemporary folk speech," give way to the poems written for Louis Zukofsky's son, Paul, poems in which Niedecker "is more than ever the shrewd aphorist." Niedecker referred to reading the February 1931 issue of *Poetry*, edited by Zukofsky and dedicated to Objectivist poetry, as an important influence on her later development. As Volkman puts it, Niedecker's later poems took on a "haiku-like tautness" that carries over "into the final collections, where terse fragments gain resonance by their contiguities within longer sequences." Throughout her career Niedecker was a poet attuned to place and sensitive to the textures of words and things.

•••

The idea for A Poetry Criticism Reader came from Jan Weissmiller. In our ongoing conversations about poetry, I periodically inquired about the progress of the reader, and at one point Jan graciously invited me to join her in the endeavor. I was pleased to accept the invitation, as I have continued to be pleased to participate in the book's development. Much of our work together on the reader involved discussing recent essays about poetry, along with making suggestions about what we might include. As it turns out, each of us is responsible for roughly half of the material here. In the end we both agreed on the full collection.

Our purpose in assembling this reader is to bring together some of the more informative essays, published over the course of the last ten years or so, about contemporary poetry. If this collection proves to be successful, we plan to oversee the production of more such volumes, published at intervals of approximately three to five years. We shall invite a different poet to choose the pieces included in each volume, thus encouraging a variety of perspectives and emphases. We trust that this, the first of our readers, will be a helpful and stimulating beginning.

In consultation with their authors, I have silently corrected minor inaccuracies in the essays, and the entire volume has been made consistent with regard to punctuation and spelling. Bracketed material within the texts is original to each essay. My own annotations appear as bracketed endnotes.

...NOTES...

1. David Perkins, A History of Modern Poetry: Modernism and After (Cambridge, Mass.: Belknap Press of Harvard University Press, 1987), p. 3.

2. Seamus Heaney, "Learning from Eliot," in his Finders Keepers: Selected Prose 1971–2001 (New York: Farrar, Straus and Giroux, 2002), p. 29.

3. T. S. Eliot, "Tradition and the Individual Talent," in his Selected Essays of T. S. Eliot, New Edition (New York: Harcourt, Brace and World, 1950), p. 4.

4. Peter Ackroyd, T. S. Eliot: A Life (New York: Simon and Schuster, 1984), pp. 31–33.

5. The occasion of the essay was Eliot's 1944 address to the Virgil Society.

6. T. S. Eliot, "What Is a Classic?" in his On Poetry and Poets (New York: Noonday Press, 1961), p. 71.

7. Eliot, "Tradition and the Individual Talent," p.4.

8. Quoted in Gerald Graff, *Professing Literature: An Institutional History* (Chicago: University of Chicago Press, 1987), p. 100.

9. Ackroyd, *T. S. Eliot*, p. 31.

10. Eliot, "What Is a Classic?" p. 53.

11. Kathy Eden, *Friends Hold All Things in Common: Tradition, Intellectual Property, and the Adages of Erasmus* (New Haven: Yale University Press, 2001), pp. 11–13.

12. See Harold Bloom, *The Anxiety of Influence: A Theory of Poetry* (New York: Oxford University Press, 1973) and *A Map of Misreading* (New York: Oxford University Press, 1975).

13. Eliot, "The Function of Criticism," *Selected Essays*, p. 12.

14. Hart Crane, "General Aims and Theories," in *The Complete Poems and Selected Letters and Prose of Hart Crane*, edited by Brom Weber (New York: Liveright Publishing, 1933), p. 218.

15. An especially helpful description of postmodern thought remains Jean-François Lyotard's *The Postmodern Condition: A Report on Knowledge* (Minneapolis: University of Minnesota Press, 1984).

16. Dana Gioia, "Tradition and an Individual Talent," in *Certain Solitudes: On the Poetry of Donald Justice*, edited by Dana Gioia and William Logan (Fayetteville: University of Arkansas Press, 1997), p. 77.

17. Hannah Arendt, *The Human Condition* (Chicago: University of Chicago Press, 1958), p. 198.

Of the Music of Poetry

...DONALD JUSTICE...

A line from Hopkins ought to be a good place to begin, for Hopkins is surely one of the most musical of poets:

Wíry and white-fíery and whírlwind-swivellèd snów[1]

This line has the same sort of flash and dash that some effects in Turner's landscapes, also of the nineteenth century, seem to have. It cannot quite be held to the literal representation of a thing, nor can a degree of the literal be wholly denied it. It can be said in this sense to be brimming with suggestion. *White*, of course, does signify in respect to a snowstorm; it is literal enough. But what of *wiry* and *fiery*? I have seen a good deal of snow in my time and have yet to see any that could be accurately described as wiry—possibly in a Japanese print featuring snow falling; nowhere else. As for *fiery*, perhaps if there were lightning in the vicinity it might apply, but this must be a rather rare weather phenomenon, and one, in any case, not mentioned in the newspaper accounts of the time on which Hopkins depended. Nor is there a possibility of fires running through the rigging of the ship, for many of the passengers sought refuge by climbing into the rigging and hanging on. We are left to guess and to gloss as imaginatively as possible. Certainty can hardly be hoped for. And there are readers of poetry who will prefer it that way. Poetry is thought to have, like royalty, its privileges, one of which is to hover perpetually just above sense, flitting and fluttering around and about, without ever being obliged to swoop and take its prey. This privilege is often associated with what is called the music of poetry, for it is just as poetry inclines toward the musical that it may excusably leave plain sense behind.

As for the music of the Hopkins line, it must, to begin with, be thought to consist of the rhyming sounds of *wiry* and *fiery*. This effect may come through as the more musical, in fact, because the rhyming sounds do not fall neatly at the ends of lines, in any set pattern, but arise suddenly and as it were accidentally, as a sort of bonus or superfluity of effect, like touches of red in an otherwise cool background. Not that a Hopkins background is ever likely to remain cool. The coincidence of these rhyming sounds with the exact point at which plain sense slips momentarily out of reach only goes to confirm the supposed musicality of the poetic moment. The sprinkling of *w*'s and *wh*'s and finally *s*'s—the ongoing ripple of alliteration—seems to bind the otherwise surprisingly discrete linguistic bits and pieces of the line more or less together, confirming and adding to what convention holds to be the music of such a line. For it is mere convention to call these effects musical, a convenience of critical language, a trope. A formula devised to account for this situation might run something like this: whenever we have x and/or y, especially in company with z, we are entitled to designate the passage as musical. X here would represent, let us say, rhyme or closeness of sound; y might be alliteration or some unusual effect of the meters; z would then be some degree of straying from any absolute requirement to make an ordinary kind of sense.

Such, in any case, would appear to be the common understanding, though normally the proposition is not put nearly so cold-bloodedly as this.

And there is no denying to the Hopkins line, indeed, to Hopkins's work as a whole—of which I happen to be very fond—a distinction of sound which is singular and most affecting: a musicality, if you must. What is baffling is that in the case of Hopkins such effects are commonly set down on the credit side of the ledger, whereas in the work of some of his contemporaries, poets like Swinburne or even the great Tennyson, very similar tricks and devices are scored against the poets. This may come about largely because Hopkins can be considered a type of the outsider, not at all the laureate type but rather the sort of romantic rebel to whom many of us automatically lend our affection, despite the odd fact that in the case of Hopkins this outsider was given to more pieties and outright moralizing than the decadent Swinburne or the laureate himself. The point is that sound effects in themselves—this sort of *texturing*—may not be enough to win admiration, though in particular cases stunning, but that they require other assumptions to validate them, assumptions about the general nature of poetry or else, culturally if not esthetically, a sort of aura about the poet or poem. For I hope we do not care for all alliteration, all midline rhymes, all peculiar or skewed diction and syntax: that would be a depraved taste indeed. Whatever sound effects we are inclined to accept will help to define and measure our taste for poetry. But guidance is hard to find through a wilderness of such effects, some intended, some merely struck off by the gods of chance (as surely some of the best must be). There are no laws ready to hand, nor should we be tempted to accept unskeptically a great deal of the law-giving handed down by some of those who have had their say on this matter. It is a tricky area, one whose trickiness ought to be more widely acknowledged.

The heart of the topic, I would argue, appears to have something to do with questions of mimesis or imitation. For as poetry is a kind of virtual speech, it becomes that by imitating speech which might actually be spoken on some occasion, if only in the privacy of one's own room, quietly and meditatively. (The other pole of language it might attempt to imitate is song, though that purpose has much less frequently been chosen in our time than speech.) There is more to imitation theory than this, but what concerns us here is the way in which the question of imitation gets involved with notions of musicality. I have proposed elsewhere[2] that the condition to which devices of sound in themselves aspire is, in any case, nonsense. Divine nonsense, perhaps, but nonsense all the same.

> Ha ha ha ha! this world doth pass
> Most merrily, I'll be sworn;
> For many an honest Indian ass

Goes for an Unicorn.
  Farra diddle dino,
  This is idle fino.

It may be that all rhymes contain a touch of nonsense, a gratuity or overflow not warranted by logic or sense and just possibly all the more pleasurable for that reason—the lucky prize at a raffle rather than the weekly paycheck—or if not nonsense strictly, then a twist of wit, involving some second or double sense. One of the reasons certain rhymes seem weaker than others, so weak as actually to offend the alert sensibility, is that this small bonus is absent.

Yet I cannot recall having seen this argument made. What we should all be tired of hearing by now is the more frequent assertion that rhyme—that any sound effect, for that matter—becomes valid insofar as it *reinforces* the sense of the passage rather than for whatever grace-note of nonsense it may introduce. This is the door by which the notion of imitation enters, and it seems to me a dreary and most Puritan outlook. Here let me quote John Crowe Ransom, who put the case fifty or sixty years ago, without apparently convincing anyone but me.

> And finally [writes Ransom] we must take account of the belief that is all but universal among unphilosophical critics, and flourishes at its rankest with the least philosophical. It is this: the phonetic effect in a poem . . . is "expressive"; that is, offers a sort of sound which "resembles" or partly "is" or at least "suggests" the object that it describes.

It is as though the theocrats and politicals of poetry could not rest until the gaiety of sound—a type of nonsense—had been pulled and twisted back into some kind of sense. Such an attitude lies behind the way a great many writers talk about poetry, particularly when they shift into analytical gear. It pervades discussions of the sound effects in poems, not only of alliteration and the various kinds of rhyme but of the meters as well. Free verse in our time has often been justified on the grounds that it better *imitates* speech than the old meters were able to, often with the additional suggestion that this is especially true of American speech, for the old meters historically are easy to associate with English ways, including what Americans could be forgiven for regarding, in some cases, as high-flown and snobbish speech. It is true that the English have shown no great genius for free verse, but this fact remains irrelevant, given the flourishing life of free verse in French, in Spanish, in Polish, in practically all modern languages, not excepting Chinese. The case for free verse would be better made on other grounds. Interestingly enough, it was Hopkins who argued, better than a hundred years ago, that his own newly invented metrical system—sprung rhythm—was superior to and more flexible than the traditional system of metering, and this partly on the grounds that it allowed for a closer approximation to the stress patterns of speech. This was true enough in certain ways. It is virtually impossible to arrange a line in the old meters so as to allow, for instance, three stressed syllables in a row, although in speech itself this gathering of stresses may occur with little enough forethought; and in Hopkins's sprung rhythm such an arrangement was not at all impossible but on occasion actively sought: "The sóur scýthe crínge, and the bléar sháre cóme."[3]

But does this sound like the speech of anyone we have ever heard speaking? Is it in fact an imitation of speech? Perhaps the speech of an impassioned minister of the gospel approaching the climax of his sermon, speech a priest might be expected to consider more natural than we would do. For most of us Hopkins's kind of "music" is Sunday speech, if speech at all, hardly the speech of every day.

Williams argued that his own free verse, some of it anyhow, aimed to imitate the very speed, the rapidity which he considered to be a property of American speech. Certainly in a poem like "It Is a Living Coral," with its short lines, there appears to be a rapidity and forward-rushing drive to the phrasing, at least when the author reads the poem for recording. But what concerns us is not whether American speech is rapid—in the South, in the period when I was growing up, it was anything but rapid—or whether it would be valuable to catch that quality in verse if it could be done, or whether in fact Williams was able to do so. What matters more for our argument is that the esthetic or theoretical basis for thinking the attempt worthwhile returns us to another aspect of imitation theory. Some idea of imitation in its various twists and turns seems to be shot through our whole way of thinking and talking about poetry, where almost any sort of possible imitation—anything from a tiny glitch of alliteration to a sweeping general impression of a nation's speech—if it can be found at all, is likely to be embraced and praised by someone.

None of this is to deny that an illusion of expressiveness sometimes envelops and hovers about a line or phrase, and poets may be pardoned for wishing to supply such grist for the critic's mill. To get such a result at times is, in any case, unavoidable, the nature of language being what it is. All the same, on investigation such illusions well may disappear: the ectoplasm proves to be an accident of developing the photographic negative and no proof of the ghost's presence. The full expressive power of poetry is not so simple as to reside greatly in sound effects. Even a metrical pattern, with its potential for variation built in, is an abstract thing, ready to become expressive through the denotation of the words and the run of sense the phrases make, but not much one thing or another in and of itself. I. A. Richards long ago cautioned that "we should not attribute to the sound alone virtues which involve so many other factors."

But might not some sort of imitation of music itself lead to what we could legitimately call music in poetry? It is a haunting thought and remains an allurement. In his introduction to *An Elizabethan Song Book*, Auden touches on the point. He suggests that the writers and musicians who put together the Elizabethan songs, out of their need to follow with words what the music was doing, discovered new and fresh metrical turns and inventions.

> THAT shall PINCH BLACK and BLUE
> YOUR white HANDS AND fair ARMS
> That DID not KINDly RUE
> Your PARaMOUR'S HARMS.[4]

The musical score dictates this placement of the stresses, a surprising and attractive dislocation, impossible to arrive at except through the musical setting. The effect is odd, special, and doubtless musical (in some sense), though we might be less certain that musical is the right word for it if we had not come across this passage in a song. What the movement of the verses here is imitating is not, strictly speaking, any sense at all, probably no identifiable emotion besides some generalized feeling of jealousy, but only a melodic line, with its own detachable rhythmic system and pattern. As Auden goes on to remark: the "words do not, as notes [in music] do, express themselves merely as sounds in temporal motion; they express their meanings as well. In music, that is, the movement is the expression; in poetry it is but a very small part of it."[5]

Both more elusive and more suggestive in its implications is Ezra Pound's now ancient credo respecting rhythm. Said Pound, conscious of taking a then revolutionary position justifying free verse: "I believe in an 'absolute rhythm,' a rhythm, that is, in poetry which corresponds exactly to the emotion or shade of emotion to be expressed."[6] The idea of such a correspondence is clearly one more version of what I have been calling imitation theory and associates readily with notions of the musical in poetry, since the musical and the expressive have generally been linked. To call what is to be expressed emotion, as Pound does, is a convenient way of referring to an otherwise unspecified subject. What this Poundian precept does encourage is a loosened meter, the broken iamb, or at least a highly flexible and free-tending treatment of the meters, on the grounds that the desired expressive correspondence would be enhanced by being more variably registered. Beyond this, the assertion, though notable, challenging, and idealistic, remains rather vague and hortatory, like other influential remarks in critical history.

In discussions of the meters, exact description and specific examples are hard to come by, especially, it seems, in discussions of free verse, for effects seem to be, except in the most general way, much harder to pin down there. Though surely nine-tenths or more of the poems written last night and every night for decades now in America and doubtless in the world at large must have been written in some kind of free verse—of course there are a thousand kinds—yet examples of the supposed effects of phonetic devices continue to be easier to come by in the older kinds of verse, especially examples specific enough to be worth fussing over and picking at. One of the strongest passages in all criticism to deal in detail with such matters, and a passage which deserves to be much better known, is—again—from Ransom, who is a great authority on such matters. The critical passage is a half-century old by now, but it is still worth looking at, considering the strange persistence of the view it pretty well demolishes. Ransom is discussing our very topic under the guise of reviewing a book on Edna St. Vincent Millay's poetry, whose author appears to have been all too bravely willing to be specific about sound effects in Millay. Here is the critic on the subject of Millay:

> Sometimes Millay gives an effect of spaciousness to pentameter by a double stress before a pause, as in
>
> On the wide heath, by evening overtaken.
>
> [Later on, with] the many f's and r's and th's a fine feeling of fluffiness is given to one line by the many unaccented syllables:
>
> Comfort, softer than the feathers of its breast,
>
> sounds as soft as the bird's downy breast feels.[7]

It would be hard to imagine a more naïvely put version of imitation theory than this; and yet it has much in common with the discussions of sound effects regularly met with in textbooks and critical articles. Ransom deals with it in this way:

> As to the effect of spaciousness caused by a double stress before a pause. Too startling is the coincidence that *on the wide heath* means spaciousness. . . . If the phrase were *in the strict tomb*, I think [the critic of Millay] would be saying that the double stress indicated crowdedness.[8]

There happens to be a popular notion, supported by T. S. Eliot and no doubt by many of those who attend readings given by foreign poets, that it is possible somehow to grasp emotionally or in some other undefined way a good part of a poem recited in a language of which the listener has no knowledge.[9] On such an occasion one might expect a double stress before a pause to produce a sensation of spaciousness in a listener who did not understand what the words were saying. Not at all likely, I should think. And it is probably just as well that sound effects are not so precisely coded. We respond more to the timbre and tone of the reader's voice, the gestures, the whole actorish character of the performance (including even the way the vagrant lock of hair is repeatedly tossed back from the forehead), and to the general reverential air of the occasion, than to any double stresses before pauses. All this is perfectly obvious, but the one thing should not be confused with and described in terms of the other. For the differences between the languages, notably as their sounds are concerned, make the translation of any sound effect from one language to another impossible, as every translator knows. This inherent impossibility is probably one of the reasons, even beyond liberal principles or the laziness of the translator, that an attempt is rarely any longer made to get the meters or the rhymes, not to mention the incidental and less patterned sound effects, into the text of a translation. If one chooses to believe in the pure expressiveness of sound, to believe, for example, that such an imitation was exact in the original language, then one must give up in advance any attempt to reproduce it exactly. Yet occasionally the translator, in an effort to achieve a general overall texturing, will substitute a certain sound effect in one place for a different sound effect in another place, as if in this realm any such sound-play might stand in as the equivalent of any other. But what does this do to the notion that a more or less exact expressiveness is ever possible by means of sound?

Ransom goes on with his demonstration:

> In the [later] example the effect is a fine feeling of fluffiness and a softness as of the bird's downy breast, while the cause is said to be the many unaccented syllables, assisted by the many f's, r's, and th's. But I will substitute a line which preserves all these factors and departs from the given line mainly by rearrangement:

> Crumpets for the foster-fathers of the brats.

> Here [says Ransom] I miss the fluffiness and the downiness.[10]

And yet perhaps there is something in all this imagined correspondence of sound and sense, even though for the most part, when examined in bald detail, it is clearly naïve and unrealistic, based on the sort of simple faith poets are not backward in encouraging, that they are wizards of the language, in control of matters more properly ascribed to chance. Of course there are mysteries and magics in composition with which the poet may hope to be in alliance, though without great hope of exercising complete control over them. As even Ransom elsewhere concedes, there is "a wonderful 'fitness,' harmony or propriety, even an enduring stability, [that] seems to obtain in the combination of the semantic property and the phonetic property into a fine poetic phrase. It is something we all feel, and I believe it is the fact we need to account for here. But what is the law of its existence?" Ransom attempts to answer this essential question in a rather philosophical manner:

> The law [he suggests] is an ontological one: the two properties shall not be identical, or like, homogenous; they shall be other, unlike, and heterogenous. It is the law of the actual world everywhere. . . . It is only the naïve prejudice of our first way of thought . . . that makes us conceive that the [semantic property and the phonetic property] must unite by virtue of their sameness.

That seems to me a most striking position, even a radical one, and directly opposed to common notions of correspondence and likeness.

In any case, the music of poetry, such as it may be, is musical only or mostly in itself, and whether it can be taken to be in some way *like* the meaning or *different* from it may finally be of little significance. In fact, it ought to be incredibly difficult to argue the point in terms of sameness and difference, since we could hardly agree on what might constitute either. I hardly think we can assign a specific meaning to most of the sound effects we spot in poems, certainly nothing like a meaning fixed and repeatable in different contexts. We must take what pleasure we can in their liberation from having to be an "echo to the sense."[11] The inability to fix such meanings is by no means tragic. Better to acknowledge that the sound effects in poems can hardly be pinned down to exactness; they keep always a bit of magic or mystery about them, something childlike and innocent perhaps, surely something attractively playful. They coexist with the meaning, not without sufficient honor of their own. Words do inevitably make sounds when spoken, or imaginary sounds when imagined; now and then it is likewise inevitable that they should gain the passing attention and even the admiration of our ear for reasons no imitation theory can account for.

Finally, the obvious needs stating. The music of music and the music of poetry are entirely different things. The rhythms of music and the rhythms of poetry have little in common. Composers have been put to considerable trouble trying to match the rhythms of text and score; often enough, particularly among contemporary composers, the choice is to override or ignore the verbal rhythms in favor of the musical. As for any of the other resources available to the composer—melody, for instance, which requires regulation of pitch—poetry affords no reasonable parallels, except in vague and hardly comparable matters of structure. With the exception of a few strained but instructive examples, such as Eliot's *Quartets*, musical structures simply do not appear in poetry. In the end the music of poetry must be understood as no more than a metaphor struck off in the heat of wishful thought.

...NOTES...

1. [From "The Wreck of the Deutschland."]

2. [See Justice's "Meters and Memory," in his *Oblivion: On Writers and Writing* (Ashland, Ore.: Story Line Press, 1998), pp. 5–12.]

3. [From "The Wreck of the Deutschland."]

4. [Thomas Campian, "Harke Al You Ladies," in *An Anthology of Elizabethan Lute Songs, Madrigals, and Rounds*, music edited by Noah Greenberg, text edited by W. H. Auden and Chester Kallman (New York: W. W. Norton, 1970; originally published under the title *An Elizabethan Song Book*, Doubleday, 1955), p. 29.]

5. [Ibid., p. xvi.]

6. [Ezra Pound, "A Retrospect," in *Literary Essays of Ezra Pound*, edited with an introduction by T. S. Eliot (New York: New Directions, 1954), p. 9.]

7. [John Crowe Ransom, "The Poet as Woman," in his *The World's Body* (Charles Scribner's Sons, 1938; reprint, with an afterword by the author, Baton Rouge: Louisiana State University Press, 1968), p. 95. Ransom is reviewing Elizabeth Atkins, *Edna St. Vincent Millay and Her Times* (Chicago: University of Chicago Press, 1936); for the passages quoted by Ransom, see pp. 238–239.]

8. [Ibid., p. 96.]

9. [For at least cognate versions of this idea, see T. S. Eliot, "Dante," in his *Selected Essays of* T. S. *Eliot*, New Edition (New York: Harcourt, Brace and World, 1964), p. 200; "The Social Function of Poetry," in his *On Poetry and Poets* (New York: Farrar, Straus and Giroux, 1957), p. 14.

10. [Ransom, "The Poet as Woman," pp. 96-97.]

11. [Alexander Pope, "An Essay on Criticism," l. 365.]

In Memory of Orpheus
Three Elegies by Donald Justice

...MARK JARMAN...

Anyone familiar with it knows that an elegiac mood pervades Donald Justice's poetry. Many of his best known poems have been written in memory of friends and relatives or to commemorate places, like Miami, Florida, and South Georgia, where he grew up and which have changed so much that to remember them instills the pain of nostalgia. The elegiac and the nostalgic are, in fact, so closely related in his poems, at times they are impossible to tell apart. None of this is news for those who know and love Donald Justice's work. I am sure that each of us has a favorite Justice poem that represents this intimate wedding of two powerful emotions. Mine is "On the Death of Friends in Childhood," from his first book, *The Summer Anniversaries*, published in 1960.

On the Death of Friends in Childhood

We shall not ever meet them bearded in heaven,
Nor sunning themselves among the bald of hell;
If anywhere, in the deserted schoolyard at twilight,
Forming a ring, perhaps, or joining hands
In games whose very names we have forgotten.
Come, memory, let us seek them there in the shadows.

Memory is invited to reencounter not only the lost friends but the lost childhood in a place made meaningful by that loss. We can find the same compelling feeling in Justice's poems about Miami and the South. This sense of loss is so perfected in Justice's work that I cannot think of another poet who has equaled his expression of it, though there are many, all in the Romantic tradition which he proudly embraces, which we might put beside him.

Having begun with the most salient and important aspect of his work—its emotional charge—I am now going to talk about something a little different. Or rather, in order to understand, perhaps, why his invitation to memory in the last line of "On the Death of Friends in Childhood" is so moving, I am going to talk about a special aspect of the elegiac that I have found in a few poems which I believe are central to Justice's work. Two of them, "In Memory of My Friend, the Bassoonist, John Lenox" and "In Memory of the Unknown Poet, Robert Boardman Vaughn," are from Justice's 1987 book, *The Sunset Maker*; the third, "Invitation to a Ghost," is included in the section of new poems in the 1995 *New and Selected Poems*. Each of these three poems alludes in some way to the life and death of the mythical musician and poet Orpheus, a figure of some importance to Justice whose newest book includes as an epigraph an epigram about Orpheus's attempt to retrieve his beloved Eurydice from death. On the dedication page of the *New and Selected Poems*, we find the following three lines:

> Orpheus, nothing to look forward to, looked back.
> They say he sang then, but the song is lost.
> At least he had seen once more the beloved back.

I hope to show that the emotive power of Orpheus's ancient story, the story of an artist's excellence and loss, as it is echoed in these three elegies by Donald Justice, provides them with some of their own emotional impact. I want to suggest as well that the role of the elegist, one Justice has taken on many times in his career, parallels the descent of Orpheus as he attempts to bring his love back to the world of the living, to retrieve what he has lost.

•••

In Memory of My Friend, the Bassoonist, John Lenox
Coconut Grove

1

One winter he was the best
Contrabassoonist south
Of Washington, D. C.—
The only one. Lonely

In eminence he sat,
Like some lost island king,
High on a second-story porch
Overlooking the bay

(His blue front lawn, his kingdom)
And presided over the Shakespearean
Feuds and passions of the eave-pigeons.
Who, during the missile crisis,

Had stocked his boat with booze,
Charts, and the silver flute
He taught himself to play,
Casually, one evening.

And taught himself to see,
Sailing thick glasses out blindly
Over some lily-choked canal.
O autodidact supreme!

2

John, where you are now can you see?
Do the pigeons there bicker like ours?
Does the deep bassoon not moan
Or the flute sigh ever?

No one could think it was you,
Slumped there on the sofa, despairing,
The hideous green sofa.
No, you are off somewhere,

Off with Gaugin and Christian
Amid hibiscus'd isles,
Red-mustached, pink-bearded
Again, as in early manhood.

It is well. Shark waters
Never did faze you half so much
As the terrible radios
And booboiseries of the neighbors.

Here, if you care, the bay
Is printed with many boats now,
Thick as trash; that high porch is gone,
Gone up in the smoke of money, money;

The barbarians . . .
                            But enough.
You are missed. Across the way,
Someone is practicing sonatas,
And the sea air smells again of good gin.

"In Memory of My Friend, the Bassoonist, John Lenox" is not Justice's only elegy for a musician, that is, if we count "Variation for Two Pianos," which recalls the pianist Higgins who has gone, taking both his pianos and leaving the entire state of Arkansas without music. There is also the fictional Eugene Bestor of "The Sunset Maker," whose entire *oeuvre* has been reduced to a single, haunting phrase remembered by the narrator. All three musicians are linked to the natural world, the one enchanted by the music of Orpheus. The birds are Higgins's pupils and Bestor's music brings to mind the landscapes of Bonnard[1] and the creation itself. When alive, John Lenox presided over Coconut Grove and the "Shakespearean / Feuds and passions of the eave-pigeons." He was possessed of a unique excellence as a "contrabassoonist," since at one time he was the only one "south / Of Washington, D. C.," but he was also an "autodidact supreme" who taught himself to play the flute. The loneliness such artistry creates is also a theme we find in these poems, and certainly it is one we can associate with Orpheus. As the critic Paul Breslin has observed in an essay in the

American Poetry Review, Orpheus is unaware of just how his music moves other people until he meets Eurydice. His love for her changes that. But after he loses her the second and final time, he immerses himself once again in his art, disengaged from the world he moves through and affects. Breslin speculates that it is for this reason that Orpheus is torn to pieces by the Thracian women. For Justice, the death of Orpheus makes the pursuit of art all the more precious.

In Justice's poetry nothing is loved so much as what is lost. In the story of Orpheus, this loss includes both Eurydice and Orpheus. And it is the latter's death, the death of the artist, that Justice depicts in these elegies. Like the head of Orpheus, borne along on the Hebrus, John Lenox is imagined sailing out "blindly / Over some lily-choked canal." He is replaced by "the terrible radios / And booboiseries" of his neighbors whose boats make a bad poetry, "printed . . . / Thick as trash," on the bay that was his kingdom. His "high porch," where he ruled creation, is gone, destroyed by greed. And the poet accuses in one elliptical phrase, "The barbarians . . ." Odd as it might seem, I think we can also hear an echo of Milton's flare of temper in "Lycidas" as he condemns the Church of England. And like Milton's Edward King, Justice's John Lenox is translated to a higher condition. He is imagined restored to youth, the genius of some South Pacific shore.

> Off with Gaugin and Christian
> Amid hibiscus'd isles,
> Red-mustached, pink-bearded
> Again, as in early manhood.

In his entry on the elegy in *The Princeton Encyclopedia of Poetry and Poetics*, Stephen Fogle observes that the form often includes "the consolation of some permanent principle." The idea of consolation may sound a religious note that, despite the echo of Milton, we do not associate with Justice. He could hardly be called a religious poet, except as he shares Wallace Stevens's affirmation in "Final Soliloquy of the Interior Paramour"—that "God and the imagination are one." Yet the absence of the Orphean Lenox is not filled in by crass substitutes alone. There is also a hint that his kind of artistry persists in the face of vulgarity. "Someone," the poet informs his lost friend, "[a]cross the way . . . is practicing sonatas." And as if to dispel the drunken aftereffects of those local barbarians and the smoke of their money, the smell of the sea air is reminiscent once again of "good" not bad gin. The endurance of the craft and charm of genuine artistry is indeed a consolation.

In Memory of the Unknown Poet, Robert Boardman Vaughn

> But the essential advantage for a poet is not, to have a
> beautiful world with which to deal: it is to be able to see
> beneath both beauty and ugliness; to see the boredom,
> and the horror, and the glory.—T. S. Eliot

It was his story. It would always be his story.
It followed him; it overtook him finally—
The boredom, and the horror, and the glory.

Probably at the end he was not yet sorry,
Even as the boots were brutalizing him in the alley.
It was his story. It would always be his story,

Blown on a blue horn, full of sound and fury,
But signifying, O signifying magnificently
The boredom, and the horror, and the glory.

I picture the snow as falling without hurry
To cover the cobbles and the toppled ashcans completely.
It was his story. It would always be his story.

Lately he had wandered between St. Mark's Place and the
    Bowery,
Already half a spirit, mumbling and muttering sadly.
O the boredom, and the horror, and the glory.

All done now. But I remember the fiery
Hypnotic eye and the raised voice blazing with poetry.
It was his story and would always be his story—
The boredom, and the horror, and the glory.

It may be a stretch to imagine the connection between a contrabassoonist and the lyre-strumming Orpheus, but the association between Robert Boardman Vaughn and Orpheus is one that Justice has made himself in another poem. In "Portrait with One

Eye," from the 1973 book *Departures* and dedicated to Vaughn, Justice addresses him playfully as "Orpheus":

Imperishable liar!
Your life's a poem still,
Broken iambs and all,
Jazz, jails—the complete works.

That poem recounts the outlandish, comical, even poetic behavior of a living individual, whose style of life seems to be a reproach to the speaker's. In contrast, "In Memory of the Unknown Poet, Robert Boardman Vaughn" is laden with a tragic sense of loss, not only of a life but of a talent. A villanelle, it has to be one of the handful—and by that I mean five or six—essential poems in the form in English. Start thinking of the others worth remembering and you'll see what I mean.

The Orpheus of "In Memory of the Unknown Poet" is a poet and not a musician, though music is still strongly associated with him. His story is "[b]lown on a blue horn, full of sound and fury." Yet the Orpheus we see here is not the witty, rakish figure of "Portrait with One Eye." This one is bereft, "[a]lready half a spirit, mumbling and muttering sadly" in the nether world of Manhattan. In this case the barbarous throng is represented by the "boots ... brutalizing him in the alley." Though the poet has lost his gift, the elegist can remember its enchantment, "the fiery / Hypnotic eye and the raised voice blazing with poetry." Ironically, Vaughn's life is "a poem still," as Justice claims it is in "Portrait with One Eye," but this poem is the one T. S. Eliot describes in the epigraph and which the villanelle employs as one of its refrains. The Orphic Vaughn, degraded to a mere ghost of himself, still embodies a story that signifies "magnificently / The boredom, and the horror, and the glory" beneath the beauty and ugliness of life.

Vaughn's fate as Orpheus is moving in part because he is obscure. Fame did not spare Orpheus, of course, but a certain obscurity is an aspect of those Justice celebrates in these elegies, as if it were part of their uniqueness, each of them, like John Lenox, being somehow "the only one." They are located in unlikely places, like Arkansas, or Coconut Grove, or in an alley in lower Manhattan, or in the case of Henri Coulette, though it is unstated, Los Angeles.

Gray's "Elegy Written in a Country Churchyard" comes to mind, in which he mourns "[s]ome heart once pregnant with celestial fire" and otherwise unknown. In a sense, Justice is bringing each of his departed friends to light, to a kind of fame. He performs an Orphean task himself by descending into that bleak underworld, the alley, where he pictures "the snow as falling without hurry / To cover the cobbles and the toppled ashcans completely," and retrieving the brutally murdered, unknown poet. His villanelle for Robert Boardman Vaughn along with "Portrait with One Eye" and the poem "Hell," from *New and Selected Poems* in which Vaughn himself speaks, recall Berryman's sequence of Dream Songs for Delmore Schwartz, another Orpheus who signified magnificently and died in obscurity.

The achievement of an artist and the loss of that achievement, the loneliness of excellence, especially excellence in obscurity, are all reflected in the life and death of Orpheus. They are conditions that move Justice and, because of his own excellence as a poet, they move us, too. I would actually like to consider sometime what it means to be moved by a poem, since emotion seems so central to Justice's poems, but I am going to assume that you agree with me about what it means. So when I say that I think the third of these elegies, "Invitation to a Ghost," dedicated to the poet Henri Coulette, is the most moving of the three, I assume you will know what I am talking about, even if possibly you don't agree.

> *Invitation to a Ghost*
> for Henri Coulette (1927–1988)

> I ask you to come back now as you were in youth,
> Confident, eager, and the silver brushed from your temples.
> Let it be as though a man could go backwards through
>   death,
> Erasing the years that did not much count,
> Or that added up perhaps to no more than a single brilliant
>   forenoon.

> Sit with us. Let it be as it was in those days
> When alcohol brought our tongues the first sweet foretaste
>   of oblivion.

MARK JARMAN

And what should we speak of but verse? For who would
    speak of such things now but among friends?
(A bad line, an atrocious line, could make you wince: we
    have all seen it.)

I see you again turn toward the cold and battering sea.
Gull shadows darken the skylight; a wind keens among the
    chimney pots;
Your hand trembles a little.
                                        What year was that?

Correct me if I remember it badly,
But was there not a dream, sweet but also terrible,
In which Eurydice, strangely, preceded you?
And you followed, knowing exactly what to expect, and of
    course she did turn.

Come back now and help me with these verses.
Whisper to me some beautiful secret that you remember
    from life.

"Invitation to a Ghost" is based in part on "The Coming Back of
the Assassinated Poet," Rafael Alberti's poem for Federico García
Lorca which begins, in the translation by Mark Strand,

You have come back to me older and sadder in the drowsy
light of a quiet dream in March, your dusty temples
disarmingly gray, and that olive
bronze you had in your magical youth,
furrowed by the passing of years, just as if
you lived out slowly in death
the life you never had while you were alive.

Adopting and reversing the strategies of poems he admires have
been techniques Justice has employed in other poems, especially
those in *Departures*. Whereas Lorca appears unbidden to Alberti and
Alberti imagines him continuing to age, even in death, Justice on
the other hand invites Coulette to return as a young man. Both
poems are also moving because they are about ghosts, so, in a
sense, their subjects are not utterly lost but still present in some
form. Contrast this with Robert Boardman Vaughn who is depicted

after the fact of his death or with John Lenox whose whereabouts are imagined vividly in some island paradise but who is inaccessible to the grieving poet. Coulette is invoked and summoned, and the poem implicitly returns both poets, himself and Justice, to their youth.

The story of Orpheus is alluded to directly in this poem, and in a wonderful passage Coulette takes on the roles of Orpheus and Eurydice both. In the penultimate stanza, Justice reminds his friend of a dream he may have had. The poignancy and tact of the following passage are characteristic of Justice.

> Correct me if I remember it badly,
> But was there not a dream, sweet but also terrible,
> In which Eurydice, strangely, preceded *you*?
> And you followed, knowing exactly what to expect, and of
> course she did turn.

Reversal, the very mechanism of irony, is a favorite strategy of Justice, as I have said. Orpheus changes places and, it appears, fates with Eurydice. This reversal and pairing may be related to the repetitions which function as a web of correspondences, like an improvised, erratic rhyme scheme, in this masterful free verse poem. Nearly a dozen of its words and phrases are repeated at least twice. As always Justice's virtuosity is subtle but unmistakable. The poem reads like a performance of one poet offered for the pleasure of another.

(Surely every Orpheus that the elegist seeks in the underworld is also a Eurydice. I have not forgotten the memoiristic poems in *The Sunset Maker* that recall Justice's music teachers, Mrs. Snow, Mrs. L, and Mrs. K.)

Orpheus must be defeated by barbarians, of course. We have seen that in the poem for John Lenox and in the villanelle for Robert Boardman Vaughn. Here they go without saying and exist outside the charmed circle of young poets Justice wishes Coulette to return to:

> Sit with us. Let it be as it was in those days
> When alcohol brought our tongues the first sweet foretaste
> of oblivion.

MARK JARMAN
...38...

And what should we speak of but verse? For who would
    speak of such things now but among friends?
(A bad line, an atrocious line, could make you wince: we
    have all seen it.)

We may or may not envy the sensitivity that would make someone
respond physically to bad poetry. And there is another threat, too,
less clear but much more ominous. Just as Orpheus descends into
hell and even, one might add, goes among the mad, murderous
Bacchantes, Coulette is depicted turning "toward the cold and battering sea" as his hand "trembles a little." This image of alienation
and annihilation takes its place darkly at the center of the poem.

I find this poem moving also because it assumes there is some
value present but secret in life. Why else would Orpheus or anyone wish to bring a loved one back from death? Whereas this secret
is identified in the villanelle as boredom, horror, and glory, and in
"In Memory of My Friend" as good music, gin, and company, in
"Invitation to a Ghost" it is simply "beautiful." My guess is that
the secret has to do with poetry and the invitation to share the
secret is based on the assumption that the dead possess knowledge
denied to the living or that the living should know but have forgotten. Orpheus descends to rescue Eurydice in order to conquer
his grief, but also for consolation, as Justice implies in his epigraph
to the *New and Selected Poems*. Though it may be essential, as T. S.
Eliot says, for the poet to see past beauty and ugliness to what lies
beneath them, it is just as necessary to believe there is some value
inherent in experience which is good or beautiful. For Orpheus as
he is embodied in John Lenox, Robert Boardman Vaughn, Henri
Coulette, and Donald Justice, this good and beautiful secret is art,
specifically music and poetry, and the work that goes into making
them, an endeavor of the living. When, in the final line of "On the
Death of Friends in Childhood," the poet says, "Come, memory,
let us seek," it is understood that the poet's means of seeking,
even in the realms of the dead, is through his poetry.

...NOTE...

1. [Pierre Bonnard, French painter, 1867–1947.]

The Elliptical Poets

...STEPHEN BURT...

"The self was once," I said, "a great, great
Glory." "Oh, sure. But is it still?"
—JAMES MERRILL, *The Book of Ephraim*

Is there a new way of looking—
valences and little hooks—inevitabilities, proba-
bilities? It flaps and slaps. Is this body the one
I know as me? How private these words?
—JORIE GRAHAM, "Notes on the Reality of the Self"

If the impersonal made personal isn't personal, then what is there?
—KAREN VOLKMAN, "Infidel"

Stephen Dobyns's best poem shows a man and his dog staring into
a refrigerator at dawn, looking for "answers to what comes next,
and how to like it." Last year a U.K. editor asked me to introduce
recent American poets to British readers—in effect, to open the
poetry fridge: I found myself surprised by how many tactics, strategies, attitudes most younger poets I liked turned out to share.[1]

Where have younger poets found themselves? Of the three mas-
ters and influences into which Vernon Shetley divides the poetry
world of the 1980s, James Merrill is no longer with us (though his
followers are).[2] Elizabeth Bishop has become part of the landscape,
no more a *direct* influence on the best new writing than Whitman.

And John Ashbery is everywhere, ramifying, still. Language writing has become for many younger writers less phalanx than *resource*, revealing a "Stein tradition" of dissolve and fracture less radical work can use.[3] Epistemology and theories of language—how we know what we know, how we say it—have become as central to contemporary lyric as psychoanalysis in the late fifties, myth and politics in the late sixties; partly in consequence, poets who invoke the line of Stevens, or of Bishop, feel free to get odder, harder, while poets who consider themselves Stein's followers sound friendlier than they once could. And Jorie Graham has become the unavoidable presence in other people's styles, partly because she teaches at Iowa and gets lots of press, but mostly because her cinematic, intellective *The End of Beauty* (1987) established her as the best poet of her contexts, the one her contemporaries have to think about.[4]

The most exciting younger poets have read Graham *and* do not imitate her; like her, they treat voice and self and identity neither as givens nor as illusions, but as problems, phenomena, poems can explore and limn. These poets share goals and tones and attitudes, and the best way to explain *what* they share is, I fear, to coin a term for a school.

•••

I therefore introduce the Elliptical Poets. Elliptical Poets are always hinting, punning, or swerving away from a never-quite-unfolded backstory; they are easier to process in parts than in wholes. They believe provisionally in identities (in one *or more* "I" per poem), but they suspect the Is they invoke: they admire disjunction and confrontation, but they know how little can go a long way. Ellipticists seek the authority of the rebellious; they want to challenge their readers, violate decorum, suprise or explode assumptions about what belongs in a poem, or what matters in life, and to do so while meeting traditional lyric goals. Their favorite attitudes are desperately extravagant, or tough-guy terse, or defiantly childish: they don't believe in, or seek, a judicious tone.[5]

Elliptical poets like insistent, bravura forms, forms that can shatter and recoalesce, forms with repetends—sestinas, pantoums, or fantasias on single words, like Liam Rector's "Saxophone":

You and I, our money. Their money.
Our pleasure and fist full of money.
Laughter over money, serious money,
over money. Too much, too little,
fluid money. The saxophone, color of wheat,
purchased through Hock Shop money, saxophone
splitting the night, our air, blowing money.

Rector's *The Sorrow of Architecture* (1984)—harsh, incisive—may be the first Elliptical book.[6] Rector's anger stems from his Brechtian interest in work, debt, and wages, in "the ongoing circulation / Of art and money . . . the hunger, // The hunt, the eat."[7] He may have invented the fractured sestina forms that pervade poems like "Driving November," a three-page work with the proportionate strength of a crime-spree film:

We are driving November we turned
October several towns back. We applaud
the passing of all that is innocent we inherit
the road as it is here. You speak of habit
as if things do not change I speak
of sweet repetition. We are driving November, from harm.

Ellipticals love poems that declare "I am X, I am Y, I am Z," where X, Y, and Z are incompatible things. Mark Levine specializes in such poems, and shares Rector's interests in money, locality, and work: Levine's debut *Debt* (1993) is Ellipticism at its most aggressive, rife with allusion and disillusion.[8] His punky "Work Song" proves him Berryman's legatee:

I am Henri, mouth full of soda crackers.
I live in Toulouse, which is a piece of cardboard.
Summers the Mayor paints it blue, we fish in it.
Winters we skate on it. Children are always
drowning or falling through cracks. Parents are distraught
but get over it. It's easy to replace a child.
          Like my parents' child, Henri.

The self Henri presents seems at once two-dimensional, replicable, disposable, even *staged*—the efficient result of a discourse—and yet he sounds like a real *speaker*, with an explosive will of his own.

Elliptical Poets treat literary history with irreverent involvement. They create inversions, homages, takeoffs on old or "classic" poems: they also adapt old subgenres—aubade, elegy, verse-letter, and especially ode. Almost all write good prose poems. Lucie Brock-Broido is the most ambitious, most tradition-conscious Elliptical. Her *The Master Letters* (1995) quarries Dickinson, Donne, *Romeo and Juliet*; exclaims, "I am angel, addict, catherine wheel—a piece of work / On fire"; specifies, "At your feet I am a shoemaker's apprentice, / Toxic in a long day of fumes"; entitles a poem "You Can't Always Get What You Want," and opens it with backtalk from *Lolita*: "Light of your loins—I have been to the ruins & come back with art."[9] Her prose poems boast menageries of similes—"senseless as crates of fish stacked glimmering, one-eyed & blank, one atop the other of them." The best of Brock-Broido's many *personae* may be Anne Boleyn, in a poem called (after Wyatt) "And Wylde for to Hold":

> Lack of water, lack of light,
> Lack of heat, lack of bedding, I should go
>
> On this way forever; it is my wont to go.
> Tonight—the wind will be high in its scaffolding,
>
> On the strength. I will listen for its habit
> Especially about the throat like an Elizabethan cuff
>
> At the crude nest of the mouth. Our bed
> Will be lined with shredded bark from sycamore & hair.
>
> Let them lie broad awake in their nest, scissoring.
> None will fly.

Ellipticals caress the technical: there is, as Rebecca Reynolds puts it, "less / [she] can touch now / that isn't technical and reluctant." They mix their affections with alienations. Susan Wheeler's *Smokes* (1998) presents her sometimes as a movie star, sometimes as a "hapless stand-in scripter" with an "impedimented personality," fleeing or seeking love or fame.[10] She, too, makes jangling leaps from low to high diction; likes to interrupt herself; writes "I am X, I am Y" poems; and mixes up old high allusions with TV and Barbies. Her special talent lies in her kidnapping of familiar forms, as in "Shanked on the Red Bed" (an update, perhaps, of MacNeice's "Bagpipe Music"):

> The century was breaking and the blame was on default,
> The smallest mammal redolent of what was in the vault,
> The screeches shrill, the ink-lines full of interbred regret—
> When I walked out to look for you the toad had left his net.
>
> The discourse flamed, the jurors sang, the lapdog strained
> its leash—
> When I went forth to have you found the tenured took the
> beach
> With dolloped hair and jangled nerves, without a jacking
> clue,
> While all around the clacking sound of polished
> woodblocks blew.

Ellipticals delete transitions: one thought, one impression, tailgates another. So did Eliot, Berryman, Hejinian; but the Elliptical fast-forward and cut-up is *way* less likely to represent speech, or stream-of-consciousness, or a program for breaking up subjects and systems; instead it's *performance*, and demonstration—if you can hear me through all this noise, I *must* be real.[11] C. D. Wright is expert at laying down a series of hints, or residues, of experience, making readers discover what happened, find their way *through to* her. Wright began publishing in the late seventies, but her best books are recent: her first fully Elliptical work is *String Light* (1991), full of detailed tenderness for, and scorched regret about, her native Arkansas.[12] She, too, has a rebellious "I" poem, "Personals":

> In this humidity, I make repairs by night. I'm not one
> among millions who saw Monroe's face
> in the moon. I go blank looking at that face.
> If I could afford it I'd live in hotels. I won awards
> in spelling and the Australian crawl. Long long ago.
> Grandmother married a man named Ivan. The men called him
> Eve. Stranger, to tell the truth, in dog years I am up there.

Wright's technique of hinting allows her in *Tremble* (1996) to make terse, radiant sketches of bodily, erotic histories, "Key Episodes from an Earthly Life": the poem of that name begins "As surely as there are crumbs on the lips / of the blind   I came for a reason."[13] It ends:

> Around this time of year   especially evening
> I love everything   I sold enough eggs
>
> To buy a new dress   I watched him drink the juice
> of our beets   And render the light liquid
>
> I came to talk you into physical splendor
> I do not wish to speak to your machine

Elliptical poets' challenging unease, their resolve neither to play by the rules nor to scrap them, extends from self and voice, through form and tradition, to grammar. "Syntax is the social aspect of language" (Donald Davie); the elliptical self, uneasily social, grows only uneasily grammatical—each distortion or shock to the syntax *means*, usually, some shock to the self. Brock-Broido, nouns verbs and dispenses with prepositions throughout the harrowing "Am Moor," an "I am X, I am Y" poem that manages to ditch the relevant pronoun: it begins, "Am lean against. / Am the heavy hour // Hand at urge, / At the verge of one." Anne Carson's newest short work belongs (as her long poems don't) in the Elliptical force field; similar syntactical slips and breaks do all the work in her "Sleepchains":

> Who can sleep when she—
> hundreds of miles away I feel that vast breath
>   fan her restless decks.
>   Cicatrice by cicatrice
>   all the links
>   rattle once.
> Here we go mother on the shipless ocean.
>   Pity us, pity the ocean, here we go.[14]

Want an Elliptical long poem? Try Wright's book-length, mostly prose *Just Whistle* or *Deepstep Come Shining*.[15] Or read Claudia Rankine's *The End of the Alphabet*, whose near-impenetrable vignettes and meta-analyses make it a sort of *Modern Love* for the post-Graham generation:

Who distributes the live or die
after juice is refused, the egg is fried?
Faced with its straggering number of runny noses
the day begins, begins again, talks above
the motor left running.[16]

But Ellipticist long poems are rare as Cubist murals: Ellipticist poems treat self and voice more or less as synthetic cubism treated shapes and things, and the poems' necessarily dense, busy surfaces make it hard for them to gain the momentum or clarity long forms can need.[17]

●●●

Is Ellipticism a school or a *zeitgeist*? Yes: let Wheeler and Brock-Broido stand for the school part, the learnable technique, at (respectively) its brittlest and most irritable, and its most extravagantly lyrical. (Both now have epigones—I won't list them—all over journals I like.) Then let the drifts in August Kleinzahler's poetry show what a wider net might hold. Kleinzahler is Elliptical in his all-inclusiveness, his casual refusals of authority, his jarring jumps from elevation to slang. Kleinzahler's wry, Californian cadences can encompass anything he sees or hears—the sun from a plane, headlines, Thom Gunn, dogwoods, crisps, DTs. A ballet he watches prompts "Sapphics in Traffic," which begins, "Festinating rhythm's bothered her axis"; where Larkin wrote "Lines on a Young Lady's Photograph Album," Kleinzahler writes the semi-rhymed, half-nostalgic quatrains of "Ruined Histories":

Ah, Little Girl Destiny, it's sprung a leak
and the margins are bleeding themselves away.
You and I and the vase and stars won't stay still.
Wild, wild, wild—kudzu's choked the topiary.

Looks like your history is about to turn
random and brutal, much as an inch of soil or duchy.
Not at all that curious hybrid you had in mind.
Jane Austen, high-tech and a measure of Mom.[18]

Thylias Moss belongs to the same *zeitgeist*, flaunts Ellipticism at its most tonally risky and socially conscious: her registers include

Blakean outrage, African-American preaching cadences, and disarming backtalk. Moss swerves between wisecracks and credos: her uneasy speakers, girls and adults, ground their defiance in local events, as in "When I Was 'Bout Ten We Didn't Play Baseball":

> It's hot. We might
> sleep on the porch. Next year we really will have it
> screened so we won't ever have to respect mosquitos
> again. I listen to all the emergencies,
> sirens of course, the Cadillac horns of the wedding, a
>   mother
> new to the area calling home her children
> forgetting not to call the names of the ones who don't
>   come
> home anymore on nights like these when all it has to be
> is summer and they're cared for better. The heat does hug.
> It isn't shy and proper. My mother wouldn't want me
> to play with it.[19]

Isn't this poem about a coherent character in a well-defined scene? Yes—but what a character! (What sentences!) And listen to "Easter" (this is the whole poem):

> Dr. Frankenstein feeds his son voltage, juice
> fires up the hormones
>
> on the day of unkillable testosterone
>
> while Mary and Martha heed their spices
> their urges to preserve, not dulled by the impropriety of the
>   kitchen
> in which slaughter lambs and chickens.[20]

Fragmentation, jumpiness, audacity; performance, grammatical oddity; rebellion, voice, some measure of closure: Ellipticist.

•••

All these extravagant, edgy writers want poems as volatile as real life; they want to remake the self, to pick up their pieces after its (supposed) dissolution. So do their peers. Most Ellipticals are between thirty and fifty, and found their real styles after 1986. If they have a geographical center, it's New York City (though several have taught, or studied, at the University of Michigan). Ellipticals invoke, as precedents, Dickinson, Berryman, Ashbery, sometimes Auden. All want to convey *both* metaphysical challenge *and* recognizable, seen or tasted, detail. Ellipticist reject: poems written in order to demonstrate theories; scene-painting, and prettiness as its own end; slogans; authenticity and wholeheartedness; mysticism; straight-up narrative; and extended abstraction (their most obvious difference from Graham). Ellipticals are uneasy about (less often, hostile to) inherited elites and privileges, but they are not populists, and won't write down to, or connect the dots for, their readers; their difficulty conveys respect.

Is Ellipticism just a name for Goldilocks's favorite porridge, neither too dry and challenging, nor too cohesively sweet? Maybe; but it seems to me that these poets, whether defined narrowly (poems that *feel and sound* like Wheeler's, like Levine's) or broadly (as far as Kleinzahler and Moss) share techniques, expectations, reactions, goals. Time will find and polish the best Elliptical verse, as it has with prevailing styles from the Tribe of Ben to the allies of Auden. I wish I had space to quote the bedazzled, lyrical prose poet Killarney Clary; Forrest Gander's careful sequences; Karen Volkman's *Crash's Law*; April Bernard's jittery *Blackbird Bye-Bye*; Reynolds's first book *Daughter of the Hangnail*; the comic, tender, botanizings and "fractal" forms of Alice Fulton; and the Ellipticals' overseas counterparts, Australia's John Tranter, who often visits the United States, and Britain's Mark Ford. For now, these uneasy, *echt* contemporary, difficult poets have written a heap of at-least-pretty-good poems. Vaunting or angry, precise but not pedantic, hip but rarely jaded, they are in all the best (and a few worse) senses, what comes next.

...POSTSCRIPT (2004)...

People who follow the arts like to talk about schools; often they prefer talking about schools and trends to talking about individual poets and their poems. The attention this essay seems to have attracted may stem as much from our collective liking for "trend pieces" (if I may steal that term from newspaper editors) as from the accuracy or inaccuracy of its claims. Writers who have taken issue with this essay either dislike the idea that any poets can ever be grouped into schools, or prefer narrower definitions of "school," or else object that it's not clear where boundaries lie.[21] Is Joshua Clover elliptical? Is D. A. Powell? Brenda Shaughnessy? Michele Leggott? H. L. Hix? Matthea Harvey? David Berman?[22]

The answers to those questions seem to me less important than the fact that they can now be asked. I aimed not to single out six or eight or ten poets as a distinct group with bright-line boundaries, but instead to describe an emerging set of styles, a family-resemblance notion, a nebula of habits and preoccupations which seemed to me then (and still seems to me now) to enfold currently influential poets (and the poets influenced by them). Ellipticism counts as a school or a movement in the way that "metaphysical poetry" or "confessional poetry" count as movements, not in the way that "language writing" or the Black Arts Movement or New Formalism (each of which had manifestos) count as movements; the so-called Ellipticals (like the so-called metaphysicals) need not have signed a manifesto, or appeared in one place at one time, in order to share the aesthetic goals I have described. (They do, however, publish in the same magazines: *Fence, Denver Quarterly, Colorado Review, Boston Review, New American Writing.*)

If "Ellipticism" in fact defines a reigning style, we might expect both the number of new adherents, and the number of limit-cases, to increase over time, at least until another style crops up to replace it. This appears to have happened. We have now, in 2004, more poetry of the sort I'd like to call Elliptical than we had in 1999 and many more first books which exhibit its features. If anything, the Elliptical style seems in danger of becoming too easy, a manner graduate students learn to adopt, then discard, before or after their first book wins an award. The growing numbers of youngish poets who might fit the Elliptical label make it easier to see what they've learned and from whom—hence easier to see which older poets might rightly define their putative school. If I were to rewrite this essay from scratch (rather than appending these belated paragraphs) I would not include August Kleinzahler, whose most disjunctive, least obviously descriptive poems now seem like outliers; younger poets have not seized on him as a model. (I sometimes wish they would.) I'm not sure I would have included Thylias Moss, though if *Last Chance for the Tarzan Holler* does not belong in this company it becomes a book with no peers and no close parallels anywhere. (That may be right.) I might have included, instead, Powell, or Liz Waldner, whose playful all-over-the-place jargon acknowledges Berrymania along with cinematic, and wholly fruitful, forms of artistic ADD. And I would certainly continue to maintain that Levine, Brock-Broido, Wright, and Carson have become influences which work *together* on many younger poets' styles (sometimes joined to the corrrosively comic influence of James Tate). These poets are trying (as Graham, more abstractly and grandly, tried just before them) to split the difference between a poetry of descriptive realism, on the one hand, and, on the other, a neo-avant-garde.

Whether a school exists, or where its boundaries lie, seem to me questions both less profound, and less durable, than the questions we can ask about each poet and about individual poems. At the same time individual poems may respond to their historical moment and invoke their stylistic affinities with other poems; if many poems do so in similar ways, they might prompt readers to class them together—to decide, even, that those poems belong to a school.

...NOTES...

1. This essay originally appeared in *American Letters and Commentary* 11 (1999): pp. 45–55; my thanks to the then editors, Anna Rabinowitz and Jeanne Marie Beaumont. Another, shorter, version of this essay appeared in *Poetry Review* (London) 88:1 (spring 1998) under the title "Shearing Away." My thanks to Douglas Wolk for telling me to invent a school, and to Jessica Bennett and Monica Youn for suggestions.

2. See Shetley's *After the Death of Poetry* (Durham, N.C.: Duke University Press, 1993), especially the introduction.

3. For how and why this could happen, see Bob Perelman, *The Marginalization of Poetry* (Princeton, N.J.: Princeton University Press, 1997), chapters 2 and 7; to watch it, delightfully, in progress, see chapter 8, "An Alphabet of Literary History."

4. Her angry detractors concede her importance, but see her as symptomatic or as opportunistic: they're quite unfair to her poems, but they, too, are part of the climate.

STEPHEN BURT

5. This rebelliousness, and this provisionality, make many of these poets sound *adolescent*, occupy the cultural position of *youth*, in ways their predecessors could not—which is a long story, fit for another place.

6. *The Sorrow of Architecture* (Port Townsend, Wash.: Dragon Gate, 1984). Will somebody please bring it back into print?

7. From his second book, *American Prodigal* (Brownsville, Ore.: Story Line, 1994).

8. *Debt* (New York: Norton / National Poetry Series, 1993).

9. *The Master Letters* (New York: Knopf, 1995).

10. *Smokes* (Providence, R.I.: Four Way Books, 1998). Check out Stephen Yenser's careful, slightly puzzled admiration for Wheeler ("Poetry in Review," *Yale Review* 87:1 [1999]: pp. 149–171) for a similar take on her aims— though Yenser goes as far afield as Michael Palmer in seeking "postmodernist" parallels.

11. Thus neither Rosmarie Waldrop nor Michael Palmer, nor Albert Goldbarth, Frank Bidart, Charles Wright—to name some talented older poets who care for epistemology and disjunction—could count as Elliptical. the first two work too far from an "I" in a real world, the other three too unproblematically close.

12. *String Light* (Athens: University of Georgia Press, 1991).

13. *Tremble* (Hopewell, N.J.: Ecco, 1996).

14. Part of the sequence "Old Home," in *Metre* 5 (1999).

15. (San Francisco: Kelsey Street Press, 1991) and (Port Townsend, Wash.: Copper Canyon, 1998).

16. *The End of the Alphabet* (New York: Grove, 1998).

17. Thus Carson's *Autobiography of Red* (New York: Knopf, 1998) explores questions about selfhood, innerness, oddity, representation, through divisions among characters and events, much more than through fissures in the language: she subordinates style to story, exactly the reverse of the way her shorter work embodies the same interests.

18. *Red Sauce, Whiskey and Snow* (New York: Farrar, Straus and Giroux, 1993); his new *Green Sees Things in Waves* is just as good.

19. *Small Congregations* (Hopewell, N.J.: Ecco, 1993).

20. *Last Chance for the Tarzan Holler* (Hopewell, N.J.: Ecco, 1998).

21. Four responses, and my response to them, follow the original essay in *American Letters and Commentary* 11 (1999): pp. 56–76; an angrier response is Steve Evans, "The Resistible Rise of Fence Enterprises" (2001), http://www.thirdfactory.net/resistible.html, last viewed 13 May 2004.

22. Yes, yes, yes, no, no, yes, and yes.

Clarity instead of Order

The Practice of Postmodernism
in the Poetry of James Tate

...JAMES HARMS...

Last year I received an e-mail message from a person I've never met in person who had just hosted James Tate for a reading and classroom visit. What struck him most about Tate, for some reason, was his antagonistic attitude toward certain academic buzzwords, namely postmodernism and theory. Tate had seemed not at all interested in discussing his poems in the jagged shadow of these terms. In fact, he claimed to be uninterested and uninvested in them.

This person I've never met in person felt Tate was being a tad disingenuous. After all, he said (I'm paraphrasing), Tate is a poet who teaches (at the University of Massachusetts–Amherst), and it's the reality of the poet's job these days to both write and theorize about writing; we're not simply writers-in-residence anymore; we're expected to know something about the discipline that's adopted us, about its discourse and vagaries. Plus, it's sort of obvious, he said (I'm wildly paraphrasing now), that Tate has waded in the waters of critical theory; I mean his poems dramatize some of the ideas postmodern criticism is investigating.

I didn't think much about this at the time. I was hip-deep (I'm going to extend the wading metaphor for a while) in Tate's latest book, *Worshipful Company of Fletchers*, and like most readers of poetry who don't also happen to be critics in the academic sense, I had reached into my closet of reading styles and extracted my Trust-First-then-Think waders, which I also use for John Ashbery and Jorie

Graham, two other poets who lead with the heart, regardless of their reputations as chilly, difficult intellectuals. In other words, I was enjoying Tate's world, which is both recognizably my own and irrevocably alien, a place where the last eland (an African antelope) can live out her days in New Jersey delivering encyclopedic monologues on the minutiae of first ladies and their nicknames, among other things ("An Eland, in Retirement"). I was enjoying myself, yes (how not to with Tate?), but I was also trying to understand. Tate's poems, as surreal as they sometimes seem, have never really been surreal; they exist in that nether region which is redolent of dreams but saturated with reality; they are "bivouacked between worlds," as he puts it in a poem from *Worshipful Company of Fletchers*[1] ("In My Own Backyard"). For that reason, it has always seemed possible to naturalize them, as if they are parables or allegories possessing codes and clues that will, if cracked, lead to the uncovering of meaning. It seems valuable to read Tate's poems this way even if it is impossible. Because part of the point of a Tate poem—which is to impose upon this master of the seemingly pointless a somewhat contradictory purpose—is to frustrate interpretation, to insist instead on a sort of surrender: to an unstable universe, to chaos enacted lovingly in language, to a perpetual present that is somehow in a permanent state of temporal flux.

In a word, to exist comfortably in Tate's world is to participate in the practice of postmodernism. We don't need to call it that, but that is what it has come to be called. And for those of us who have long suspected (perhaps long feared) that postmodernism is, in fact, more a practice than a theory, it makes perfect sense that after a period of relative neglect, James Tate is suddenly one of our most honored poets. Like Ashbery, he has been writing for years about a life we never knew we were living, or perhaps never wanted to know we were living. And as if in anticipation of some sort of paradigm shift in consciousness that has engendered a vastly different way of being in the world and in the moment, James Tate has been deliberately (if anyone so playful can be called deliberate) crafting a body of work that dramatizes what some critics have described as the postmodern breakthrough—a turning away from the perhaps outmoded ambitions and anxieties of modernism to an embrace of uncertainty and a valorization of play, a world of suspensive irony, to use Alan Wilde's term as explained in Brian McHale's *Constructing Postmodernism* (London: Routledge, 1992): "Where the characteristic 'disjunctive irony' of modernism sought to master the world's messy contingency from a position above and outside it, postmodernist suspensive irony takes for granted 'the ironist's immanence in the world he describes' and, far from aspiring to master disorder, simply accepts it" (21). This is by no means an ironclad description of Tate, who can seem quaintly romantic and vividly modern at times. But then again, one of the tenets of postmodernism is that it preserves as much it rejects.

Certainly Tate privileges the subjective imagination as dutifully as any romantic, as anxiously as any modernist. But he seems to be making no argument in the process, or as the postmodern theorist might say, he is compelling no consensus. In Tate's cartoon universe the subjective is exaggerated into the purely personal without ever calcifying into statement—dramatic situations are decontextualized while remaining recognizable, so that historical pressures and societal strictures are still present, if somehow denatured and neutralized. I offer the title poem from *Distance from Loved Ones*, in its entirety, as example:

> After her husband died, Zita decided to get the face-lift
> she had always wanted. Halfway through the operation
> her blood pressure started to drop, and they had to stop.
> When Zita tried to fasten her seat belt for the sad drive
> home, she threw out her shoulder. Back at the hospital
> the doctor examined her and found cancer run rampant
> throughout her shoulder and arm and elsewhere. Radiation
> followed. And now, Zita just sits there in her beauty parlor,
> bald, crying and crying.
>> My mother tells me this on the phone, and I say:
> Mother, who is Zita?
>> And my mother says, I am Zita. All my life I have been
> Zita, bald and crying. And you, my son, who should have
>> known me best, thought I was nothing but your mother.
>> But, Mother, I say, I am dying. . . .

JAMES HARMS
...54...

What to do with this poem? The first paragraph (I'm taking this to be a prose poem, though it's difficult to be certain) compresses a tragedy to the point where it becomes nearly absurd, enough so that we find ourselves challenging the existing narratives we carry around in our heads to cope with such situations. The shift in point of view in the second paragraph problematizes the poem further. It requires a revision of our relationship to the subject, since, subtly, the subject is beginning to shift from Zita to the first person narrator; if nothing else, the sudden presence of the narrator in the poem complicates our feelings for Zita by complicating her as a character. The poem then jettisons the literal and asks that we reinterpret the dramatic situation metaphorically, nearly allegorically. As if this weren't enough, the speaker reasserts himself as the poem's subject in the final line and leaves us with very little more than ambivalence, a very strange emotion to process after the presumed pathos of the opening paragraph.

In other words, we have in this poem, as we do in so many of Tate's, a narrative that is strangely out-of-time and off-balance, that purposely resists the larger metanarratives that we've come to expect from the heroic tradition of western poetry, those grand and organizing principles that are usually there, if only between the lines. As McHale puts it in discussing Lyotard, metanarratives are those "various stories (Enlightenment, Marxist, Hegelian) about human emancipation and progress that once served to ground and legitimate knowledge, [and which] are no longer credible."[2] And as I've suggested, Tate is also very good at invalidating the smaller narratives that construct our belief systems and attitudes of response, those stories we've come to believe about the enduring nature of the human animal.

So, to return to Tate's fascinating recent poem "An Eland, in Retirement," we find ourselves listening to a strangely slippery voice, one that begins in the third person with a matter-of-fact description of the eland (which quickly degenerates into absurdity) then abruptly shifts into the first: we come to find that it is the eland herself who is speaking the poem. In this way Tate calls attention to the whole concept of persona and creates what might seem to be a symbolic voice for the individual (as opposed to the actual voice of an individual him/herself). And though certainly this voice is on some level bitter and alienated in the best modern fashion (after all, she is the very last of the elands "and nobody cares"), we're never far from laughter while listening to it, never able to completely accept the authenticity of the utterance, since Tate isn't interested in creating an individuated character. Rather, the self-consciousness of the poet and his foregrounding of artifice (the sublime absurdity of a talking eland who in all other ways resembles the last of the frustrated and lonely American spinsters) force an adjustment of expectations: we're not going to ever know what the eland stands for, what her story means. She may sound like us and act like us, but that doesn't mean she can tell us who we are. Regardless, there's the temptation of interpretation—even as we laugh—when the last eland recounts her travails with the opposite sex; certainly this is the self-consciously self-analytical American consumer, forced to shop for companionship and, furthermore, forced to shop outside of her neighborhood:

> I have, for the record, agreed
> to three "dates" since the last of my kind passed on:
> the first was with an impala; it had a very attractive
> purple-black blaze on its forehead, and moved
> with great grace, but finally it was too jumpy.
> It would jump ten feet over nothing, and this seemed to me
> entirely unnecessary and unnerving. The second
> was a disaster: a wildebeest by the name of Norman.
> Norman would run around in circles snorting,
> tossing his head as if it were on fire.
> My last attempt at finding a mate is better left untold.
> A bat-eared fox. I was desperate, and temporarily
> lost all sense of decorum, for which I am truly chagrined.
> He was cute, a fine pet, perhaps, but hardly
> a suitable father for my progeny.
>
> (Worshipful Company of Fletchers)

As a sort of absurdist lampoon of contemporary mores and customs, this has some impact, especially in its wild asides on the medicinal properties of egg noodles and lobster, which come earlier in the poem. But it doesn't hold together well; the voice of the eland is never really recognizably a single voice, never really a singular presence, and as a result, the possibilities for absurdist satire very quickly disintegrate. This is because the individual consciousness in a Tate poem is not convinced of her own alienation or estrangement, never fully sure of her marginalization. She would have to be at odds with the chaos of the surrounding culture to feel that way. Instead, she accepts herself less as a unique and solitary being (ironic in this case, since she's the last eland) than as a prism, her individuality as much a function of refraction as invention. She is a trivia collecting eland come to live out her life in America, or a voice created by trivia that might as well be an eland.

This is where chaos quite pleasantly enters the picture. Tate's poems splash happily in their zaniness, in their slipping attempts to tell their stories using devices and conceits that simply don't hold together. We see this dramatized brilliantly (and somewhat frighteningly, certainly irreverently) in "How the Pope Is Chosen," also from *Worshipful Company of Fletchers*. The conceit in this poem is aggressively foregrounded and hilarious. Simply put, Tate discusses popes using terminology normally applied to poodles. What is disturbing, not to mention uncomfortably familiar in its reflection of postmodern consciousness, is the way the potentially satiric extended metaphor continually falls apart and reinvents itself, carried along by the momentum of the activity of inventive refraction (details from popular culture are everywhere present in the poem, and entirely generative) more than by any sort of intent or meaning, any sort of thematic and satiric pursuit. This is how the poem begins, and where, in part, it goes:

> Any poodle under ten inches high is a toy.
> Almost always a toy is an imitation
> of something grown-ups use.
> Popes with unclipped hair are called *corded popes*.
> . . .
> Popes are very intelligent.
> There are three different sizes.
> The largest are called standard Popes.
> The medium-sized ones are called miniature Popes.
> I could go on like this, I could say:
> "He is a squarely built Pope, neat,

well-proportioned, with an alert stance
and an expression of bright curiosity,"
but I won't. After a poodle dies
all the cardinals flock to the nearest 7-Eleven.
They drink Slurpies until one of them throws up
and then he's the new Pope.

Why does the slip and shift in the extended metaphor—that moment when Tate seems to almost accidentally use the vehicle when he should be using the tenor,[3] where the terms of the metaphor are suddenly weirdly complicated by the drinking of Slurpies (not exactly poodle-like behavior)—why does it disturb as much as delight? In some ways, the answer to that question legitimizes this whole enterprise, this need—if we can call it that—to talk about Tate's poems in these terms. After all, isn't it enough to simply applaud and enjoy the way this utterly unique and distinctive poet allows us to insinuate our own needs on the denaturalized landscape of his poetry without confronting the strained and increasingly inauthentic specter of autobiographical veracity? Certainly part of his appeal has to do with a turning away: from the pessimistic confessions of contemporary poetry, from the demands of the intimate voice, from the plainspoken truths that emerge from logical arguments. Without abdicating responsibility for language and its determinacy, Tate provides relief from delimited meaning and its various vehicles.

And yet, like Ashbery and Graham, like Michael Burkard and Ralph Angel and Lyn Hejinian and Brenda Hillman and countless other fine poets who defy easy explication without sacrificing beauty, James Tate *provides* with his poetry, even if what is provided is largely ineffable. His is a language of acceptance, of embrace, a peculiar variation on Whitman's inclusiveness, since Tate's democracy of details seems not to respect the historically imposed values of linear organization. Tate's universe is uncontainable and his sense of time and space favors simultaneity instead of sequentiality. That moment of slippage in "How the Pope Is Chosen" is a crack in the fortress, the fortress being the poem as a representation, however associatively constructed, of an understandable existence. It is a self-conscious gesture that breaks the plane between writer and reader, that subverts the rhetorical design of the metaphor, that willfully mocks any willing suspension of disbelief. What Tate's poetry desires is clarity, not order, and in that way it seems suddenly braver and more honest than a poetry that attempts to explain or italicize or even simply reify. As he states himself in a poem from Constant Defender, "If I am some sort of nut who spends his life / elaborately avoiding what I like best, / let it be clear."[4]

But as for that person I've never met in person, and his encounter with Tate . . . I can imagine what happened very clearly: It's an afternoon class, and the students have been asked to prepare questions for the guest of honor. After a few fairly harmless queries—Do you write with a pencil, a pen, or on the computer? How much do you revise? Do you try to be so funny or does it just sort of happen?—someone, perhaps even the teacher, innocently asks, Do you consider yourself a postmodernist?

I can see Tate scowl just a bit, his face falling first then rearranging itself into a weak smile. "Post what?" he says. "Is that some sort of cereal? Does it have raisins?" He turns then to the next question.

The more I think about this scene (which, admittedly, is more my invention than any reported fact) the more I am reminded of my high school marine science class. My teacher, Mr. Stellern, explained to us the theory of plate tectonics—this was in 1977 or so. "They call it a theory," he said, "but that's baloney. It's happening. It's for real." I didn't think much about it at the time, just as I hadn't first given much attention to Tate's reaction to being labeled a postmodernist. But now I imagine my brother, who was a geologist for several years, climbing down into the San Andreas Fault, turning to the west and asking the Pacific Plate, "So, do you consider what you're doing—all this slipping and shaking—plate tectonics?"

"Call it what you like," the plate answers. "I've been doing it for years."

...NOTES...

1. [James Tate, Worshipful Company of Fletchers (Hopewell, N.J.: Ecco, 1994).]
2. [Brian McHale, Constructing Postmodernism (New York: Routledge, 1992), p. 5.]

3. [For an explanation of the terms "tenor" and "vehicle" in relation to the analysis of metaphor, see I. A. Richards, *The Philosophy of Rhetoric* (New York: Oxford University Press, 1936), pp. 95–112.]

4. [James Tate, "If It Would All Please Hurry," in his *Constant Defender* (New York: Ecco, 1983).]

On Paul Muldoon's *Hay*

...JOSHUA WEINER...

Getting a poem by Paul Muldoon into your mouth is a bit like eat-
ing spaghetti with a spoon—one can't decide whether the task requires a heads-down shoveling technique or a delicate balancing
strand by strand. Muldoon's fondness for alternating long and
short lines of heavily enjambed free verse coupled with an often
prosaic syntax forces a reader to speed up in order to sustain the
sentence, while the poet's proclivity for end-rhyme forces one to
slow down. The effect is a contrived awkwardness, a kind of formal clowning around that keeps one off-balance, rhythmically and
syntactically tipped forward and correspondingly yanked back.
Reading such poems takes some practice, but one's attentiveness
is rewarded with definite pleasures. Some of this pleasure comes
from hearing within a whacked prosody the fragments of a prior
poetry, the way you can hear a folk ballad behind one of Bob Dylan's
surreal dream songs; and it is precisely the echo of an ancient
ancestral form shading a contemporary idiom that lends expressive resonance to Muldoon's postmodern ironies. Consider the
opening of "The Mudroom," the first poem in Muldoon's new
book, *Hay*:

> We followed the narrow track, my love, we followed the narrow
> track through a valley in the Jura
> to where the goats delight to tread upon the brink

of meaning. I carried my skating rink,
the folding one, plus
a pair of skates laced with convolvulus,
you a copy of the feminist Haggadah
from last year's Seder. I reached for the haggaday
or hasp over the half door of the mudroom
in which, by and by, I grasped the rim
not of a quern or a chariot wheel but a wheel
of Morbier propped like the last reel
of *The Ten Commandments* or *The Robe.*

While the endearment, "my love," comes across as pastiche, the shifting rhythm of the first two lines (iamb to anapest) acts as the formal synapse of a cultural memory that sparks the connections between a parody of pastoral tradition, postwar Judaism, Anglo-Saxon millery equipment, antique technology evoking a "heroic" age, and the biblical mythologies immortalized by Hollywood. A healthy amount of the verse movement and end-rhyming here, as elsewhere in *Hay*, suggests a brainy brand of doggerel, a ragged yet inventive rhyming that seems less an act of ideational yoking than a contemporary conceit for a mental process of homonymic association in which disparate elements are brought together by virtue of an intelligence attuned to the mere sound of things. Many of Muldoon's poems are a replica of a mind containing multitudes—diction from different worlds of experience, books, movies, music, cities, mythologies, high and popular culture. A mind that works along such zigzagging routes of association naturally spins rather convoluted narratives, though the motivation behind such impulses often seems at the service of creating an occasion to construct the network rather than tell the story (this at a time when we seem to take as much pleasure in the serendipity of the network as we once did in an elegantly turned dramatic frame). Muldoon is thus one of poetry's darling plateau-jumpers, finding spring in qualities of diction, a ranging historical consciousness, rich allusiveness, and quickly shifting attention. He often conveys in his work a subversive sense of fun bursting from a pervasive gravitas, as if he were the kid in school who watched the most television, set the curve, and kicked ass in the orchestra.

JOSHUA WEINER

And one of the great pleasures in reading Muldoon's work is keeping attuned to the channel-changing of these musical, culturally patterned networks. As a formal process, the poem demands that you keep the whole verbal object in mind as you read along the linear path, for any prior word or phrase can change into any future word or phrase in a continual revolution of the poem as kaleidoscope. Such a mapping extends as well to the book as a whole, particularly with the poem "Errata," which asks that you mentally search and replace particular words occurring throughout the book ("For 'Antrim' read 'Armagh.' / For 'mother' read 'other.' / For 'harm' read 'farm.' / For 'feather' read 'father.'") It is up to the reader to remember the location of each "mistake" and trace the implications of the "correction." The pervasive sense of the poem's vertical as well as horizontal movement, the necessity for the reader to keep every word and phrase in mental play, suggest that Muldoon is inventing a new spatial form for the postmodern poem. I mean postmodern here in the sense that Muldoon self-consciously rejects the heroic struggle of building a monument. Even as his vast and unpredictable word hoard and delight in verbal invention seem Joycean (and even as Joyce himself parodied the epic), Muldoon never attempts to build a verbal edifice according to a master plan; rather, one feels his verbal patterns are clusters that could replicate themselves in an endless improvisation as he delights, like that goat, in treading upon the brink of meaning. He is, in formal sensibility, our most Ovidian poet, whose talents in this respect are most impressively displayed in the long poem "Yarrow" from his previous volume, The Annals of Chile, in which a sense of psychological obsession seems to drive the poem. In Hay we find it again in the last poem, "Bangle (Slight Return)." Here a heroic battle from antiquity becomes superimposed on Muldoon's personal heritage and the present drama taking place in a Parisian restaurant:

> Even now my da and that other jolly swagman would rake
> their horses over the manganese-bright stones
> and into the canebrake.
> That streel of smoke. That tink of blade on bone.
> The Greeks' al-al-al-al-alalaes

as they fought hand-to-hand
under the shadow of Troy's smoke-blackened walls.
Until there again, as if wounded, she threw up her right hand

and I glanced the glance of one of those kookaburras
through the canebrake, the kookaburra that laughs last,
and I heard her laugh

as I continued to peruse
the dessert menu cum wine list,
every so often turning over a new coolibar leaf.

In the section following, the bright stones will turn into a suitcase, the smoke will hang ambiguously between the fires of an ancient battle site and a smoking cigarette in the contemporary scene, only to become further refigured in the poem's unfolding. The sequence is made up of thirty such "sonnets," though there could've been a hundred, one feels, spun out with the facility of Merrill Moore[1] composing rapidly at a traffic stop. Muldoon rides easily on the vitality of his own making that, even in grappling with often violent historical subjects, gallops with an irrepressible joy and buoyancy.

It's peculiar, then, considering Muldoon's forte with the extended poetic series, that the form would also reveal his greatest weaknesses in two of the book's longest poems, "Sleeve Notes" and "Hopewell Haiku" (each about twenty pages). "Sleeve Notes" is a personal, sometimes cryptic, history of the poet as a young man, revealed in flashes that are themselves connected in the poet's mind to particular rock albums. The title of each poem bears the title of each respective album, from "The Jimi Hendrix Experience: *Are You Experienced?*" to "Van Morrison: *Astral Weeks*" to "Leonard Cohen: *I'm Your Man*," and the like. Sometimes the poem comments directly on the music, sometimes not. Most of the time, the result seems distracted, attenuated, lightweight—one can't really call it light verse, as the poems lack snap, crackle, or pop. A few of them contain the genuine sense of mystery and surprise that has become Muldoon's signature, as with this two-liner on the eponymous Dire Straits album: "There was that time the archangel ran his thumb along the shelf / and anointed, it seemed, his own brow with soot."

"Hopewell Haiku" takes the form of another kind of personal journal, of the poet's domestic life during a New Jersey winter amongst family and pets. There are ninety of these, hit and miss, some quite striking in their figurative elegance (for example: "A stone at its core, / this snowball's the porcelain / knob on winter's door"). Some are jokey: "Though cast in metal / our doorstop hare finds no place / in which to settle." Or: "A horse farts and farts / on the wind-tormented scarp. / A virtuoso." Perhaps I should confess an impatience with this vision of settling down, seemingly so relaxed in its Dockers, a kind of wry East Coast version of Robert Hass's poems of California, mired as they sometimes are in cuisine. Muldoon expresses such satisfactions with a characteristic self-reflexiveness as well, as when he compares himself in "Sleeve Notes" to Warren Zevon, "whose hymns to booty, to beasts, to bimbos, boom boom, / are inextricably part of the warp and woof / of the wild and wicked poems of *Quoof*" (the title to his fourth book). Muldoon's appreciations of his benign and mundane life in Hopewell are attractive for adhering strictly to the formal demand of haiku while eschewing any vestiges of orientalism; yet Muldoon's sensibility, so charged by a literary wit, can't help but make a parody of the form—the Chaucerian farting horse, for example, joined to the Romantic elevation of "wind-tormented scarp" shows off wit in spades, but the mind here seems trapped in culture.

Elsewhere it is in just such an arena of culture and history that Muldoon's performances attain a profound virtuosity. In "Aftermath," for example, three sections, each four to six lines, juxtapose sites of torture and destruction, the bloody toast, "let us now drink," acting as the common vocal refrain between them: a hanging, in which a body appears "wired up to the moon," a corpse with "the skin of his right arm rolled up like a shirtsleeve," and a torched house, for which "we knew there would be no reprieve / till the swallows' nests under the eaves / had been baked into these exquisitely glazed little pots / from which, my love, let us now drink." The convention of a patriotic victory toast combined with a chilling casualness and truly brutal aestheticism display Muldoon's gift for heightening artifice into a dark illumination.

As Yvor Winters pointed out in the work of Mina Loy, Muldoon often fuses the imagist poem to the epigram (they also share an ear for neologism and the weird, archaic word). Take "White Shoulders": "My heart is heavy. For I saw Fionnuala, / 'The Gem of the Roe,' 'The Flower of Sweet Strabane,' / when a girl reached down into a freezer bin / to bring up my double scoop of vanilla." There is an old school delight in that slippery sexual conceit, charged anew by the obliquely slanted end-rhyme, aerated syntax, and ironic allusiveness. For all his pop-culture inclusions, Muldoon remains a thoroughly literary poet, though one senses that he finds in mass media and mall life the kind of energies that attracted the Romantics to folk idioms and the Augustans to pagan cultures. If he sometimes seems to roll more than he rocks, this reader remains thankful for a growing body of work that is helping to keep the art of poetry alive—its past as well as its future.

...NOTE...

1. [A poet early associated with the Fugitive Agrarians, Merrill Moore produced sonnets numbering in the tens of thousands. In his prefatory statement to M: *One Thousand Autobiographical Sonnets* (New York: Harcourt, Brace and Company, 1938), Moore attests to having written 50,000 sonnets, though he assures the reader that most will not be published. In his "Merrill Moore: A Comment on His 'American' Sonnet" (ibid.), Louis Untermeyer writes that Moore "has written as many as a hundred [sonnets] in a four-hour period."]

On Jorie Graham's *Swarm*

...STEPHEN YENSER...

Jorie Graham's *Swarm* is abuzz with beginnings and rife with endings. To complicate matters, more than most volumes it asks to be read all at once. In this regard it is akin to other determinedly experimental, metaphysically ambitious, spiritually aware, eclectically informed, obsessively revised, and self-consciously subversive projects. If T. S. Eliot's *Four Quartets* were to collide with *The Waste Land*, the debris pattern might look like this. Among recent books, Frank Bidart's *Desire* and Michael Palmer's *Sun* share qualities with *Swarm*—qualities that appear earlier in David Jones's *Anathemata*, which Graham credits in her mercifully selective endnotes, and the work that made these others possible, Ezra Pound's *Cantos*. An aggregate of perceptions, reflections, monologues in the voices of mythical characters, and glosses on other works in a variety of free verse forms, *Swarm* seems to want to have no edges, no boundaries, no unchanging shape. When we read in the book's penultimate utterance (like most others here, it is not a complete sentence) of "the atom / saturated with situation," we have to remember "the atom still there at the bottom of nature" in the first poem and all of the references to atoms between. "More atoms, more days, the noise of the sparrows, of the universals" is one of Graham's vividly disconcerting attempts to summarize at once the world—from its simplest component (at root *atom* means "not cut" or in Graham's formulation "already as little as it can be") to its comprehensive and axiomatic principles—and this collection.

This book's universe (everything "turned into one") is a congregation of mixogamous bits each "saturated with situation" or thoroughly imbued with its context—though the concept of "context" might have to be altered: "Bless, blame, transvaluate— / Change context— / Unexpect   context," she counsels us in "Eve"—so that as in a swarm of bees the distinction between unicity and multiplicity seems irrelevant. "To swarm," the jacket copy reminds us, "is to leave an originating organism—a hive, a home country, a stable sense of one's body, a stable hierarchy of values—in an attempt, by coming apart, to found a new form that will hold." If that rather overbearing definition leaves the species *Hymenoptera* in its rapidly broadening wake—the wake of the *Arbella* and its flotilla might come to mind instead—it nonetheless suggests the behavior of these poems. As in her earlier *Region of Unlikeness*, St. Augustine supplies the epigraph to this volume ("To say I love you is to say I want you to be"), and it might be that in conceptualizing its "swarm" we should think also of the description of God sometimes attributed to him as a circle whose center is everywhere and whose circumference is nowhere.[1] Graham's "Prayer," an unusually straightforward poem indebted to Friedrich Hölderlin, ends with these lines: "I called you once and thought you once. / You travel down to me on your allotted paths, // a light embrace, miraculously omnipresent."

In any case God is relevant. The first poem in *Swarm* presents itself as a fragment "from The Reformation Journal," and its title's religious overtones are soon reinforced. The poem begins with a bold statement as to how to read this book. As in *The End of Beauty*, where she numbered them, Graham separates her lines, in this case with extra leading and sometimes an asterisk:

> The wisdom I have heretofore trusted was cowardice, the
>   leaper.
>
>   *
>
> I am not lying. There is no lying in me,
>
>   *
>
> I surrender myself like the sinking ship,

a burning wreck from which the depths will get theirs
   when the heights have gotten theirs.

My throat is an open grave. I hide my face.

I have reduced all to lower case.

I have crossed out passages.

I have severely trimmed and cleared.

Locations are omitted.

Uncertain readings are inserted silently.

Abbreviations silently expanded.

A "he" referring to God may be capitalized or not.

A rejection of her mode hitherto—which had been increasingly disjunctive but which she now wryly views as retrograde and cowardly and identifies with "the leaper," a figure that would be appropriate in George Puttenham's nomenclatorial inventions in *The Art of English Poesie* (where we find other terms we could adapt to advantage here, including *the trespasser, the straggler,* and *the disabler*)—this passage outlines the new aesthetics, the reformation of the poet.

The new aesthetics springs from the Augustinian motivation to confront candidly whatever the case may be. Although we might find it hard to trust a statement such as "There is no lying in me," Graham certainly intends no irony—nor is she, I think, disingenuous. Regardless of whether she can possibly vouch for her own honesty, her claim implies an ambition and sets a standard. The aim is that of the aggressive spiritual exercise. Graham has not yet quite eliminated all humor from her poems, but the grim irony of the fourth line quoted earlier is about as funny as she gets (she asks near the book's end, "what do I do with my laughter"), and for the most part she is engaged in a struggle so strenuous that it makes one think of Jacob, teeth gritted, as it were, muscles bunched, bearing down as though in childbirth. And let the reader beware: to approach this book in good faith you must commit yourself to some version of the same agon. There are no extended luscious passages here, no spacious pastoral interludes in which you can loaf and invite your soul, no discursive retreats, no plots grassy or otherwise to fall back on. Indeed, there are precious few uninterrupted sentences. Some time ago Graham seems to have taken literally Pound's advice to "Leave blanks for what you do not know," and here her implicit ignorance joins with a certain *askesis* to produce as *hard* a text as I have encountered recently. One has to get at it in a new way—a way roughly analogous to that in which one first got at John Berryman's *Homage to Mistress Bradstreet* or Emily Dickinson's more elliptical poems in their manuscript forms. Some poets need to devise a language within the language.

The Dickinson poem Graham alludes to and says in an endnote "animates the book throughout" is number 640 in Thomas Johnson's edition of *The Complete Poems.* As Graham informs us, the title of her "For One Must Want / To Shut the Other's Gaze" misquotes the fourth stanza of Dickinson's poem, one of her fiercest proclamations of love in separation. In the original, "One must wait / To shut the Other's Gaze down," but that verb is evidently not avid enough for Graham. The situation of the Dickinson poem, however, is to Graham's purpose. Beginning "I could not live with You— / it would be Life— / And Life is over there," it addresses a lover who eclipses the deity: "Your Face / Would put out Jesus'," Dickinson blasphemes, and

> You saturated Sight—
> And I had no more eyes
> For sordid excellence
> As Paradise.

Because of the ruinous potential of the love,

> We must meet apart—
> You there—I—here—
> With just the Door ajar

That Oceans are—and Prayer—
And that White Sustenance—
Despair.

Graham's poem, whose imagery harks back to that of the ship-
wreck in the opening lines of the book, is a dark night of the soul
in which she reflects on her predecessor's plight and her own:

What are you thinking?
Here on the bottom?
What do you squint clear for yourself
up there through the surface?

Explain   door ajar.
. . .
Here: tangle and seaweed
. . .

Explain   saturated.
Explain   and I had no more eyes.

Whether Dickinson's problematic poem is ultimately religious
or not, Graham's must be, in the sense that it reiterates the search
for the God mentioned at the outset. God also appears, I take it,
in another guise with Dickinsonian connotations: "A wise man
wants? // A master," Graham admits in "Underneath (9)," and then
later in "Underneath (Always)":

But, master, I've gone a far way down your path,
emptying sounds from my throat like stones from my
    pockets,
emptying them onto your lips, into your
ear warm from sunlight
Not in time. My suit denied.

Not in time: Graham uses the phrase three more times in the ten
lines following. The echo of Eliot's phrase in "Burnt Norton" has
here two senses: the quester is too late, as it were, yet it is precisely only "not in time" (outside time, that is) that she can be successful. Near the end of her book, speaking as Eurydice, the poet
still asks, "where is my master? with whom share death?"

Graham casts her search in psalmic terms in "Probity," in one of the simplest passages in the volume:

> I have shown up sweet lord
> have put my hand out
> have looked for a long while
> have run a hand along
> looked for a symbol at the door
> a long while
> devices   prejudices
> have felt for the wounds
> have tired eyes

But they also might not be served who stand and wait. In Graham's relationship, too, there is still that "Door ajar / That Oceans are—and Prayer" between the two principals. Like Thomas the doubter she has "felt for the wounds," but unlike him she has been neither satisfied nor shamed. To be sure, the "sweet lord" she seeks does not always resemble Jesus. She also identifies deity with "atoms" (the "saturated" motif is just one link between the meditation on Dickinson and the book's opening and closing poems) and "universals." But whatever deity is, it has to do with telos, which has to do with death. In "Underneath (8)" the devastating possibility is put like this:

> As in they shall seek death
>
>   ⋆
>
> and shall not find   it
>
>   ⋆
>
> What if there is   no end?
>
>   ⋆
>
> What if there is no
>
>   ⋆
>
>   punishment.
>
>   ⋆
>
> As in   it is written.

God has to do, as that last phrase hints, with narrative. The speaker's search is a journeying across a "Desert / Dune," as one poem is called, a pursuit as by ghost riders over a wasteland ("invisible crowd, dust-risen faces . . . then cooling sand, then crack of voices riding by, // some laughter ticked-out over sand, // deeper and deeper into the open") of "the seriously wounded narrator" (not the poet, nota bene), who would be the author of "the true story" ("Underneath [9]"). The Fisher-King also puts in appearances as Odysseus, Agamemnon, Oedipus, Lear, and others, while Graham's "invisible crowd" recalls the "crowd [that] flowed over London Bridge," and perhaps also, in a book called Swarm, "those hooded hordes swarming / Over endless plains." But Graham's story is more fragmented than Eliot's.

It is at this point precisely of story, of narrative, that writing and teleology intersect. To write consistently in full sentences and in lines without lacunae or to provide a "true story" would be for the poet to collude in the creation of the fable of purpose and unity. To break the sentence is to admit that the sentence is: to be broken. ("What if there is no // * // punishment?" What if Thomas cannot be shamed? The pun on sentence is featured, along with related others, in "Fuse," in which the speaker is the Watchman in the beginning of Aeschylus's Agamemnon who waits, alone and seemingly interminably, for the lighting of the last in a chain of beacons that relay the news that Troy has fallen. "It is a sentence   the long watch I keep," because until the watch is ended, it is a kind of punishment. The fragmented sentence is the sentence levied upon the Watchman. Later he tells us that, waiting for the "syntax" of signal fires to complete itself, he is "Always drowsy. Never spelled." ("Thy word is all, if we could spell,"[2] George Herbert exclaimed. What if the beacon is never lit?) "Dear   sentence   so filled with deferral": the apostrophe is the Watchman's and the poet's. The grammatical sentence beginning thus is itself never completed but after forty lines frays out in several directions and in this respect seems to refigure the book. Of course to the extent that the sentence is a life sentence, its conclusion can only be in death. Maybe death bestows meaning, in short—but it might also be that there is no end, no purpose. Perhaps "Chance replaces punishment," as the last poem hypothesizes. In other words, "Explain accident," as Graham has it elsewhere.

One of the crucial accidents in Swarm repeats an event recorded in Region of Unlikeness in a poem called "The Phase after History."

The first indication of it in this volume is in the second poem, "Try On":

> Wings thickly lifting off the hidden
> nest.

> The sound of a hand-sized stone hitting dry ground
> from a certain height.

Other inchoate references appear now and again, and then more than fifty pages later, in "Underneath (1)," they all come into focus:

> Painful to look up.
> No. Painful to look out.

> Heard the bird hit the pane hard.
> Didn't see it. Heard nothing
> drop.

> To look out and past the shimmering screen to the miles of
> grasses.

Now when we look back through such small foreshadowings as "Wrecks left at the bottom, yes. // Space   birdless" to that first mention, and to its anticipation in "I surrender myself like the sinking ship, // * // a burning wreck," the poem coheres around the image of the bird—probably a sparrow, because sparrows appear elsewhere in *Swarm*, so that Hamlet's meditation on accident and providence[3] is drawn into the orbit of the image, which image also helps to account for another rich phrase, repeated three times, in the opening poem: "glassy ripeness." Whatever else these words signify, they could refer to the instant of the bird's death in the collision with the windowpane. *Glassy* might glance at Paul's promise in 1 Corinthians 13 to the effect that we shall one day, instead of apprehending God as through a glass darkly, see him face to face, and *ripeness* might well call up Edgar's pronouncement in *Lear* ("Men must endure / Their going hence, even as their coming hither: / Ripeness is all"[4]), and in any event we will reflect on Graham's insistent if always undermined conjunction of death and revelation. As she has it in her concluding poem, in almost her last words,

STEPHEN YENSER
...74...

The woman of clay;
I wanted to be broken, make no mistake.
I wanted to enter light—and everywhere its mad colors.
To be told best not to touch.
To touch.
For the farewell of it.

The speaker is in part Mary Magdalene wanting to touch the risen Christ ("Noli me tangere," he warns her), but she has read the later *Cantos*. In "Canto XCII," for instance, Pound beseeches "Lux in diafana, / Creatrix," that his daughter be able to "walk in peace in her basilica, / The light there almost solid"—and we find an "invisible basilica your willingness its floor" in Graham's "Daphne," where she also writes "Let light come into   taste light," as well as "light touching everything / grace and slenderness of its touching" in juxtaposition with "to make the basilica of divine hazard" in her "Underneath (Upland)." If, earlier in this same poem, which is "Underneath (Calypso)," we might suspect another more eccentric allusion to Ezra Pound, especially since, according to his *donnée* he is the Odysseus to whom Calypso speaks—

Why should the exile   return home?
Era?   Period?

—we might be forgiven on the basis of the dense intertextuality of the book, which is in the end not a collection of poems or a sequence, really, but indeed a swarm.

Images comparable in structural importance to that of the bird abound in the book. In a longer essay one could follow among others the changes rung on the "door ajar," veils, empire, mirrors, and conjunctions of ear and mouth. That is the nature of *Swarm* as one warms to it: it's busy as bees, coherent but uncontainable, on the move, unpredictable, part of a process, and always reforming itself. The wineglass shattered underfoot in the Jewish wedding ceremony portends wholeness. For her part, Graham is deeply antinomian, perhaps philosophically anarchist, but never chaotic. She is grammatically and punctuationally promiscuous in the service of fidelity to a kaleidoscopic vision of things as she thinks they are, things that again remind us of Hopkins, things

variegated   dappled   spangled   intricately wrought
complicated   abstruse   subtle   devious
scintillating with change and ambiguity

Graham's final lines (which might allude to Michelangelo's paint-
ing of Adam's initial human movement as well as to Eve's trans-
gression and Mary Magdalene's impulse) are as follows:

To be told best not to touch.
To touch.
For the farewell of it.
And the further replication.
And the atom
saturated with situation.
And the statue put there to persuade me.

Statue derives, of course, from a root meaning "to stand, to be
placed, to be erected," while *persuade* comes from words having
to do with sweetness, pleasure, enticement. Graham's book concludes—pauses, rather, on a threshold—with an emblem sonorously, sensuously saturated with inception.

...NOTES...

1. [It may be that this metaphor of the infinite circle—in some instances it
is the infinite sphere—has come to be associated with St. Augustine because
of R. W. Emerson's misattribution at the beginning of his essay "Circles."
Clarence H. Miller, who carried out an extremely helpful e-correspondence
with me concerning the metaphor, assures me that several proximity searches
in the *Patrologia Latina* database turned up no occurrences of this description of God in the writings of St. Augustine. As Stephen Yenser helpfully
points out, the metaphor occurs in Pensée 72 of the edition of Pascal's *Pensées* edited by H. S. Thayer and Elisabeth B. Thayer (New York: Washington
Square Press, 1965). The Thayers note that the metaphor was a commonplace description of God or Being among medieval theologians. One can find
a very early instance of the metaphor in the second definition recorded in
the *Liber XXIV Philosophorum* (*Book of 24 Philosophers*), at one time attributed
to Hermes Trismegistus. The history of the metaphor interested Jorge Luis
Borges; see his "The Fearful Sphere of Pascal," *Labyrinths: Selected Stories &
Other Writings* (New York: New Directions, 1964). See also Karsten Harries's
"The Infinite Sphere: Comments on the History of a Metaphor," *Journal of*

the *History of Philosophy* 13:1 (January 1975), which is written in part as a response to Borges.]

2. [George Herbert, "The Flower."]

3. [See 5.2.215–220 in *Hamlet*, edited by Harold Jenkins, The Arden Shakespeare (New York: Methuen, 1982), p. 407.]

4. [See 5.2.9–11 in *King Lear*, edited by R. A. Foakes, The Arden Shakespeare (New York: Methuen, 1997), p. 363.]

Some Notes toward a Poetics

...LYN HEJINIAN...

...1...

Poetics is not personal. A poetics gets formed in and as a relationship with the world.

Poetics is where poetry's engagement with meaning as meaningfulness gets elaborated—poetics is the site of poetry's reason—where the plurality of its logics and the viability of its contexts are tested and articulated.

A poetics considers how and what a specific poem means within itself and its own terms and how and why it means (and is meaningful) within a community that congregates around it—around it as writing in general and around certain specific writings and writing practices in particular.

I espouse a poetics of affirmation. I also espouse a poetics of uncertainty, of doubt, difficulty, and strangeness. Such a poetics is inevitably contradictory, dispersive, and incoherent while sustaining an ethos of linkage. It exhibits disconnection while hoping to accomplish reconnection.

...2...

Aesthetic discovery can be congruent with social discovery. Aesthetic discovery occurs through encounters, at points of contact, and so too does political and ethical discovery.

These points of contact or linkages are the manifestation of our logics; they give evidence of our reasoning and they also serve as the sites of our reasons—our reasons to do what we do.

...3...

At points of linkage, the possibility of a figure of contradiction arises: a figure we might call by a Greek name, *xenos*. *Xenos* means "stranger" or "foreigner," but more importantly, from *xenos* two English words with what seem like opposite meanings are derived: they are *guest* and *host*.

A guest/host relationship comes into existence solely in and as an occurrence, that of their meeting, an encounter, a mutual and reciprocal contextualization. The host is no host until she has met her guest, the guest is no guest until she meets her host. In Russian the word for "occurrence" captures the dynamic character of this encounter. The word for event in Russian is *sobytie*; *so* (with or co-) and *bytie* (being), "being with" or "with-being" or "co-existence." Every encounter produces, even if for only the flash of an instant, a xenia—the occurrence of coexistence which is also an event of strangeness or foreignness. A strange occurrence that, nonetheless, happens constantly—we have no other experience of living than encounters. We have no other use for language than to have them.

...4...

The guest/host encounter creates "a space of appearance"—which in classical Greek thought constitutes the polis, the place, as Hannah Arendt puts it, for "the sharing of words and deeds." Arendt continues: "The polis . . . is the organization of the people as it arises out of acting and speaking together, and its true space lies between people living together for this purpose, no matter where they happen to be."[1]

She goes on to make a further and very important point: "To be deprived of it means to be deprived of reality, which, humanly and politically speaking, is the same as appearance. To men the reality of the world is guaranteed by the presence of others, by its appearing to all; 'for what appears to all' [says Aristotle in the *Nichomachean Ethics*], 'what appears to all, this we call Being.'"[2]

An apparent opposition arises here, between the ancient Greek political notion that reality exists in and as commonality, which in turn establishes communality versus the contemporary (though century-old) aesthetic notion that the commonplace and the habituation that occurs within it produce a dulling of reality, which it is the business of art to revitalize or revivify.

But it is a false opposition, one that is resolved within the treasuring of living, that is valued as the dearest thing in life by both ancients and moderns. We have always wanted things to be real, and we have always wanted to experience their reality since it is one with our own.

The notion that the world is common to us all is vital. We need the world—which is to say all things need all other things; we all need each other—if we are to exist as realities. As George Oppen puts it in his poem "A Narrative": "things explain each other, Not themselves."

Reality consists of all that is the world that is common to us all; and it is inextricably related to the space of appearance, the polis.

A valuable contribution to this notion of the polis is contained in Charles Altieri's characterization of the creative ground and its citizen, the creative self: the creative ground is "a source of energy and value in the objective order that otherwise mocks subjective consciousness"; the creative self is one "whose activity discloses or produces aspects of that ground which have potential communal significance. Art becomes a social and cultural force and not some form of individual therapy or self-regarding indulgence in the resources of the individual's imagination."[3]

...5...

Along comes something—launched in context.

That something is occurring means it is taking place, or taking a place, in the space of appearance.

It is almost automatic to us to assume that this *something* (on the one hand) and *we* (on the other) exist independently—that *something* was independently elsewhere (out of sight and mind) prior to coming into the zone in which *we* perceive it and which we, at the moment of this perceptual encounter, designate as context. Furthermore, it is at the moment that we perceive this something that we ourselves come into that context—into our coinciding (by chance?) with something. The context, in other words, is the medium of our encounter, the ground of our becoming (i.e., happening to be) present at the same place at the same time. By this reasoning, one would also have to say that context too is launched— or at least that it comes into existence quâ context when something is launched in such a way as to become perceptible to us and thereby to involve us—whomever we are—strangers (even if, perhaps, only momentarily strangers) to each other previously and now inseparable components of the experience.

As strangers (foreigners), it is hard for us to find the "right words" (themselves simultaneously demanding context and serving as it) for what we experience in that perception and involvement.

Usually comparisons are the first things foreigners make. "The dark castle on the hill is like a cormorant on a rock stretching its crooked wings in the sun" or "The pink wet light in Saint Petersburg on a winter day is like a summer San Francisco fog," etc. Such comparisons, reaching out of the present situation to another, previously experienced, recollected one, may appear to constitute the "making of a context" for the current context, but a context made in such a way is a transported one, acquired by way of metaphor. And such metaphors, cast in the form of similes and intended to smooth over differences, deny incipience, and to the degree that they succeed, they thereby forestall the acquisition of history.

But the phrase or sentence "Along comes something—launched in context" announces a moment of incipience; one could even say that it is itself, as a phrase or utterance, a moment of incipience. Something that wasn't here before is here now; it appears and it appeared to us, and it is acknowledged by the sensation *this is happening*.

...6...

I would like now to introduce a notion that Heidegger (in "On the Way to Language") terms "propriation." "Language lets people and things be there for us," he says, meaning language's proper effect, the effect of propriation.

Language grants (acknowledges, affirms) and shows (or brings into the space of appearance) what it grants: each utterance is a saying of the phrase "this is happening."

As Goethe says (in lines quoted by Heidegger): "Only when it owns itself to thanking / Is life held in esteem." "To own" here is used in the sense also of "to own up," which is to give oneself over, to experience hospitality, *xenia*, the guest/host relationship. And to enter the relationship of xenia is to accept its obligations. "Every thinking that is on the trail of something is a poetizing, and all poetry a thinking," says Heidegger. "Each coheres with the other on the basis of the saying that has already pledged itself . . . , the saying whose thinking is a thanking."[4]

To propriate, then, is to grant, to acknowledge, to own up, to love, to thank, to make a hospitality bond with.

This is intimately connected to poetic uses of language. In Greek culture, as you know, the *symbolon* was a token representing xenia— a token broken in half and divided between guest and host to be carried as proof of identity that could be verified by comparing its other half—a token by which a stranger becomes a guest.

The word as symbol establishes a guest/host relationship between speaker and things of the world. We are strangers to the things of which we speak until we speak and become instead their guests or they become ours. This transformation of the relation in which two beings are strangers to each other into a relation in which they are guest-host to each other is propriation.

"Propriation is telling"[5]—a speaking that matters. We tell in order to become guests and hosts to each other and to things—or to become guests and hosts to life.

...7...

I want to bring forward another Greek term, *thaumzein*: *thaumzein* names our great wonder that there is *something* rather than *nothing*, our "shocked wonder" (to quote Hannah Arendt) "at the miracle of Being."[6]

This is an incipient experience for philosophy as for poetry, both of which are excited into activity by *thaumzein* and the perplexity that comes with it.

Hannah Arendt locates it in what she calls natality—beginning, the highly improbable but regularly happening coming into existence of someone or something. Here, in a unique and singular happening, commonality too comes into existence. One thing that is common to us all is that we are born; another is that we are different from each other. Singularity and commonality are the same occurrence, and this condition of natality remains with us. Human lives, as Arendt says, are "rooted in natality in so far as they have the task to provide and preserve the world for, to foresee and reckon with the constant flux of newcomers who are born into the world as strangers."[7]

To be rooted in natality means that humans are born, and to be born is to become the beginning of somebody, "who is a beginner him[or her]self."[8]

"[M]en [and women], though they must die, are not born in order to die but in order to begin."[9]

To begin has two senses: one gets begun and one causes beginnings. "The new beginning inherent in birth can make itself felt in the world only because the newcomer possesses the capacity of beginning something anew, that is, of acting."[10]

...8...

To value the new was, of course, a widely held and explicit tenet of modernist aesthetics, as in Pound's often cited commandment, "Make it new." Viktor Shklovsky's more thoughtful, more self-reflexive, and better analyzed aphorism—"In order to restore to us the perception of life, to make a stone stony, there exists that which we call art"[11]—takes the behest further, making newness not an end in itself but a strategy employed for the sake of the enhancement of experience, and as an affirmation of life. "Only the creation of new forms of art can restore to man sensation of the world, can resurrect things and kill pessimism."[12] Shklovsky goes on, of course, to elaborate a now familiar set of devices intended to restore palpability to things—retardation, roughening, etc.—that are major elements (and, in ways that can be taken as troubling, even the stock in trade) of so-called innovative poetry to this day (eighty-three years later). Contemporary poets—myself among them—have embraced this project. Comments variously repeating or attempting to extend Shklovsky's proposition appear throughout my teaching notebooks:

> Language is one of the principal forms our curiosity takes.
> The language of poetry is a language of inquiry.

SOME NOTES TOWARD A POETICS

Poetry takes as its premise that language (all language) is a medium for experiencing experience. It provides us with the consciousness of consciousness.

To experience is to go through or over the limit (the word comes from the Greek *peras*—term, limit); or, to experience is to go beyond where one is, which is to say to be beyond where one was (the prepositional form *peran*, beyond).

Imagine saying that at one stage of life, one's artistic goal is to provide experience (new or revivified, restored to palpability) and at another (later) it is to provide the joy of that experience.

After how much experience can one feel free of the fear that one hasn't lived (the fear of an unlived life)?

It is the task of poetry to produce the phrase this is happening and thereby to provoke the sensation that corresponds to it—a sensation of newness, yes, and of renewedness—an experience of the revitalization of things in the world, an acknowledgment of the liveliness of the world, the restoration of the *experience* of our experience—a sense of living our life. But I do not want to imply that to produce such a sensation is necessarily to produce knowledge nor even a unit of cognition; rather, its purpose is to discover context and, therein, reason.

Admittedly, several obvious (and boringly persistent) problems arise when *experience* is assigned primacy of place in an aesthetics and its accompanying discourse of value—when it is given the status of final cause and taken as an undisputed good. First, giving preeminence to experience would seem to demand what is termed "authenticity."

Happily, one can debunk this on the same basis that one can debunk a second problem, which I could describe as anti-intellectual and ultimately philistine. In assuming a positive value to experience for its own sake, and in advocating thereby an art that heightens perceptibility, one risks appearing to privilege sensation over cogitation, to promote immediacy and disdain critique. There is a danger of implying that the questioning of experience may serve to distance and thereby diminish at least aspects of it, and that this is antithetical to "real" artistic practice. This is the basis of art's supposed hostility to criticism, theory (thought), and occasional hostility even to examination of its own history. Or, to put it another way, on these grounds, the philistine romantic attempts to ground his or her rejection of context.

And here is the basis for a dismissal of these two related problems. One cannot meaningfully say "This is happening" *out of* context. At the very moment of uttering the phrase, "natality" occurs. And from that moment of incipience, which occurs with the recognition of the experience of and presented by the phrase *along comes something—launched in context* through the phrase *this is happening,* we are in context, which is to say, in thought (in theory and with critique) and in history.

There is no context without thought and history. They exist through reciprocation of their reason. Otherwise, there is no sensation, no experience, no consciousness of living. And, to quote Tolstoi just as Shklovsky does: "If the complex life of many people takes place entirely on the level of the unconscious, then it's as if this life had never been."[13]

...9...

And here I'll introduce one last Greek term: *eudaimonia,* which is often translated as happiness, but more accurately it means "a flourishing."[14] *Eudaimonia* is what the Greeks called the sheer bliss of simply being alive. *Eudaimonia* is the joy one experiences in the mattering of life—in the sufficiency of its matter. It is pleasure in the fact that it matters.

It is matter with history, not so much because it has a past as because it cares about the future.

What "matters" must be concerned with what will come to matter: the future. We care about the idea of what's going to happen to humanity. If we didn't, life would be meaningless. If we knew the world was going to end, we wouldn't be willing to continue. To flourish in the present requires requiring, which is to say, the future. *Eudaimonia* literally means to be "with a demon"—eu-daimonia— one "who accompanies each man [and woman] throughout . . . life, who is his [or her] distinct identity, but appears and is visible only to others."[15] This daimon is the future.

As writers, we care for and about the future; we make it matter.

I can only agree with Viktor Shklovsky when he says that "the creation . . . of art can restore to [us] sensation of the world, [it] can
resurrect things and kill pessimism."[16]

...NOTES...

1. Hannah Arendt, *The Human Condition* (Chicago: University of Chicago Press, 1958), p. 198.

2. Ibid., p. 199.

3. Charles Altieri, *Enlarging the Temple* (Lewisburg, Penn.: Bucknell University Press, 1979), p. 33.

4. Martin Heidegger, *Basic Writings*, edited by David Farrell Krell (New York: HarperCollins, 1993), p. 425.

5. Ibid., p. 420.

6. Arendt, *Human Condition*, p. 302.

7. Ibid., p. 9.

8. Ibid., p. 177.

9. Ibid., p. 246.

10. Ibid., p. 9.

11. Quoted in Viktor Erlich, *Russian Formalism* (The Hague: Mouton Publishers, 1955), p. 76.

12. Viktor Shklovsky, "Resurrection of the Word," in *Russian Formalism: A Collection of Articles and Texts in Translation*, translated by Richard Sherwood, edited by Stephen Bann and John E. Bowlt (Edinburgh: Scottish Academic Press, 1973), p. 46.

13. Leo Tolstoi, in his diary on 1 March 1897, quoted by Viktor Shklovsky in "Art as Technique," in *Russian Formalist Criticism*, translated and edited by Lee T. Lemon and Marion J. Reis (Lincoln: University of Nebraska Press, 1965), p. 12.

14. [See Gerard J. Hughes, *Aristotle on Ethics* (New York: Routledge, 2001), pp. 22–24.]

15. Arendt, *Human Condition*, p. 193.

16. Shklovsky, "Resurrection of the Word," p. 46.

A Lament in Three Voices

...HELEN VENDLER...

...I...

At times, a poem is so powerful that it bursts the bounds in which it was written—the bounds of language, geography, epoch. The notorious modern case is The Waste Land—an untranslatable poem, one might have thought, except that it has been universally translated, universally read, and universally—strange though it might seem—understood. Coming upon a poem of that degree of power is a revelatory experience. Thanks to Czeslaw Milosz, born in 1911, and his translator, the poet Robert Hass, another such poem, Milosz's A Treatise on Poetry[1]—new to us, though written in 1955–1956—is appearing in English for the first time.

English-speaking readers of Milosz have been tantalized since 1988, when Milosz's Collected Poems was published, by the brief five-page excerpt in that volume from a long poem called A Treatise on Poetry. Somewhere in Polish, we realized, there nestled a hidden store of thoughts on poetry by one of the great writers of the twentieth century. What did such a treatise say of the prewar twentieth century of Milosz's youth? Of poetry, in Poland and in the world? Of the war that Milosz saw at firsthand in Nazi-occupied Warsaw? Of art in general? Of the obligations of the artist? Of modernist theory? Of the connection between political matter and aesthetic form? We knew, from other poems and from his essays and interviews, that Milosz was concerned with all these questions—

but we still could not read the dryly named poem that might embody his most intense verse-reflections on them.

Now we have the whole *Treatise*, translated by the poet Robert Hass, and accompanied by Milosz's incisive historical and ideological notes (first published in the recent Polish reissue of the *Treatise*). To enter the current of this poem is to hurtle downstream through history on a flood of eloquent and passionate language that is in turn philosophic, satiric, tender, angry, ironic, sensuous, and, above all, elegiac. At the time of writing the *Treatise*, Milosz, at forty-four, was living a life of extreme uncertainty, financial insecurity, and emotional strain. He had burned his bridges with his native country four years before, when, as the first secretary at the embassy of the People's Republic of Poland in Paris, he had asked for political asylum in France. This was a catastrophic act for a poet, since a poet's self is inseparable from his language; and Milosz did not fit easily into Polish nationalist émigré society in Paris, where he was regarded with suspicion as a former diplomat of the Communist régime. It was in this time of dislocation and desolation that Milosz turned to a fierce questioning of his own past and that of literary Poland, writing the *Treatise* at the height of his poetic powers.

I quote from Robert Hass's brief outline, in his "Translator's Note," of the four cantos of the *Treatise*:

> The first section of the poem, "Beautiful Times," describes Kraków and the condition of Polish culture at the turn of the nineteenth century [Milosz's subtitle is *Kraków, 1900–1914*]. The second section, "The Capital," describes Warsaw [1918–1939] and makes an assessment—almost poet by poet—of the state of Polish poetry in the first three or four decades of the century, particularly of its failure to account for the reality that overwhelmed that city. The third section, "The Spirit of History," on the war years [1939–1945], is a meditation on the nature of history, on language and raw force. . . . The fourth section [1948–1949] makes a startling leap. The war is over. The narrator is sitting in a boat on a lake in northern Pennsylvania, waiting for a vision from the books of his childhood: a hoped-for glimpse of the American beaver. It is a meditation

on nature, on Europe and America, and the role of the poet in the post-war world.

Such a brief account of a half-century—Krakow in the Belle Époque; literary Warsaw in the prewar years; Nazi-occupied Warsaw in the time of war; nature in the postwar New World—reveals the matter, but not the manner, of Milosz's alternately austere and torrential poem.

It is useful, then, that Hass's subdivisions help us to appreciate Milosz's varying choices of manner. There are, first, the poet's un-expected changes of focus. We see the "beautiful times" of Krakow in 1900—its monuments, its poets, its newspapers-on-a-stick in the coffeehouse, its waiters:

> Cabbies were dozing by St. Mary's Tower.
> Kraków was tiny as a painted egg
> Just taken from a pot of dye on Easter.
> In their black capes poets strolled the streets.
> Nobody remembers their names today,
> And yet their hands were real once,
> And their cufflinks gleamed above a table.
> An *Ober* brings the paper on a stick
> And coffee, then passes away like them
> Without a name.

This passage reveals the traits characteristic of Milosz's imagistic renderings of history: the sharp miniaturization of a city to an egg; the elegiac present-day note struck in "Nobody remembers"; the intense focus on an engraved detail ("their cufflinks gleamed"); the almost unnoticed glide of the past tense into the present; and the stealthy slide from the present of action into the eternal pres-ent of the vanished—"their cufflinks gleamed . . . An *Ober* brings the paper . . . / . . . then passes away like them / Without a name." As the poet seesaws between 1900 and 1955, we feel his imagina-tive unrest in the fluctuation of details, as the diminutive scale of the egg yields to the human scale of the poet, as the "real" past is obliterated by the mention of "today," as the tenses melt and diverge.

• • •

As for "Part II: The Capital, Warsaw, 1918–1939," here, Milosz's unwieldy task is to chronicle the labor it takes to drag a nineteenth-century literature of Romantic Polish nationalism into modernity. "In Poland," he says, "a poet is a barometer." He enumerates the failed strategies resorted to even by poets he admired, when they struggled with the social reality of Poland after World War I:

> There had never been such a Pléiade!
> Yet something in their speech was flawed,
> A flaw of harmony, as in their masters.
> The transformed choir did not much resemble
> The disorderly choir of ordinary things.

Here are three such poets, described, like the others, in Milosz's brief verse-sketches—in truth, epitaphs. The first poet, Jan Lechón, author of a 1918 poem "Herostrates" (named after the arsonist of Artemis's temple), decides to turn away from history to nature but subsides into nostalgia; the second, Antoni Slonimski, vows himself to an Enlightenment rationalism which he sees vitiated by political violence; the third, Julian Tuwim, a visionary embarrassed by his own visions, lapses into conventional thinking. All three poets are finally trapped in cul-de-sacs of their own making:

> Lechón-Herostrates trampled on the past.
> He wanted to see green spring, not Poland.
> Yet he was to meditate all his life
> On Old Poland's dress and antique manners. . . .

> What of Slonimski, sad and nobleminded?
> Who thought the time of reason was at hand,
> Giving himself to the future, proclaiming it
> In the manner of Wells, or some other manner.
> When the sky of Reason had grown blood-red,
> He gave his waning years to Aeschylus.

> [Tuwim] aspired to long poems.
> But his thought was conventional, used
> As easily as he used assonance and rhyme,
> To cover his visions, of which he grew ashamed.

From particular writers, Milosz turns more generally to groups; the avant-garde poets are dismissed for having subsided into a decadent and emasculated doctrine of art-for-art's-sake tinged with a retrograde nationalism. And then, bafflingly, there were the Stalinist poets indifferent to the crimes of Stalin, represented here by Lucjan Szenwald, "a Red army lieutenant" who, in spite of his repellent beliefs, wrote good poems:

> Poetry has nothing to do with morals,
> As Szenwald, a Red Army lieutenant, proved.
> At a time when, in the gulags of the north,
> The corpses of a hundred nations whitened,
> He was writing an ode to Mother Siberia,
> One of the finer Polish-language poems.

As Milosz catalogues the spirit in which a frustrated modernism struggled for expression and found it either partially or not at all, he suggests his own bewilderment when, as a young man, he was looking for convincing aesthetic models and finding the available ones inadequate to his desires. But then, as war erupts in Europe, his life is changed forever, and his art as well.

•••

At this point, A Treatise on Poetry erupts, too. The leisure for prewar retrospect allowed in Part I, the literary inventory permitted in Part II, cannot survive under bombardment. In the searing "Part III: The Spirit of History: Warsaw, 1939–1945," a new barbaric primitivism erases all of culture—art, law, literature, architecture. The canto opens with nine bleak and scathing lines in which, by a relentless ritual antiphony of "When" and "Then," civilization is undone:

> When gold paint flakes from the arms of sculptures,
> When the letter falls out of the book of laws,
> Then consciousness is naked as an eye.
>
> When the pages of books fall in fiery scraps
> Onto smashed leaves and twisted metal,
> The tree of good and evil is stripped bare.

When a wing made of canvas is extinguished
In a potato patch, when steel disintegrates,
Nothing is left but straw huts and cow dung.

Some will be reminded here, as the technology of war meets the landscapes it lays bare, of Anselm Kiefer's fallen wing on a stubble field, a version of that twisted pastoral evoked also by Paul Celan, who, in his "Deathfugue," evoked the golden hair of Faust's Margarete with the hair-turned-to-ashes of the incinerated Shulamith. Milosz's nine-line overture opens the themes of Part III: How to write the history of war? How to describe the unspeakable events of the Polish war years, including the destruction of the Warsaw ghetto?

The wrath of History takes Warsaw in its grasp, and Milosz's manner imitates the chaos of incommensurate detail as ordinary life persists side by side with war. Death inhabits the market along with chickens and geese. Nobody pays attention to dying Jews. The river flows on as before. The usual smugglers ply their boats taking depth soundings. Church bells ring over crematoria. This is the atmosphere perceived by Milosz's Hegelian Spirit of History; it exhibits the meaninglessness and disorder that he finds at the core of his own experience and that serves him as the cauldron of a new reality. Milosz rises to his best panoramic and fragmented style in creating the landscape for his Hegelian phantom:

Chickens cackle. Geese stretch their necks from baskets.
In the town, a bullet is carving a dry trace
In the sidewalk near bags of homegrown tobacco.
All night long, on the outskirts of the city,
An old Jew, tossed in a clay pit, has been dying.
His moans subside only when the sun comes up.
The Vistula is gray, it washes through osiers
And fashions fans of gravel in the shallows.
An overburdened steamer, with its smugglers' load,
Churns up white froth with its paddlewheel.
Stanislaw, or Henryk, sounds the bottom with a pole.
"Meter." Chlup. "Meter." Chlup. "Meter Twenty."

Where wind carries the smell of the crematorium
And a bell in the village tolls the Angelus,
The Spirit of History is out walking.
He whistles, he likes these countries washed
By a deluge, deprived of shape and now ready.

It is worth stopping on such a passage—Milosz's take on the
moment when the world becomes psychically unmanageable—to
see how the poet conveys its disorder. The account is full of common things: chickens, geese, osiers, bell. It sketches in the con-
tours of the old village—the sidewalk, the Vistula, the church
tower—and mentions a clay pit at "the outskirts of the city." It
confirms the continuation of immemorial habits—the marketing,
the recitation of the Angelus. It even records the poet's inveterate
recognition of aesthetic moments: the river "fashions fans of gravel
in the shallows" as it washes through the reeds. But in the midst
of these ever-familiar things, new and horrible facts have to be ac-
commodated in the mind: the bullet making its incision; the vic-
timized and dying Jew; the sound of moaning; the smell of burning
bodies. The habit of noticing aesthetic detail, chillingly, goes on
unabated: the look of the "dry trace" of the bullet—a sight unseen
before—has to find its verbal formulation.

Milosz's manner here—as he uses a panning lens, stopping
punctually for a moment at each sight—abandons cause and effect
for a set of indigestible and grammatically equal sentences. His
sequence of thoughts—this; that; the other—declares the impossibility of any logical subordination, rational hierarchy, or even
intelligibility: "Everything only connected by 'and' and 'and'"—as
Elizabeth Bishop said despairingly of history in "Over 2000 Illus-
trations." It may seem irrational to remark, between bullets and
corpses, on the beauties of the Vistula, to record that the bullet
makes its unfamiliar trace near "bags of homegrown tobacco." Yet
how else can a writer be faithful to the reality of war, which may
change very few things and yet change everything? Milosz, never
a poet to shade the truth, is willing to present, uncensored, this
panorama of the empirically undeniable, to record "the disorderly
choir of ordinary things": and for that very reason the Spirit of

History is revealed to him, whistling appreciatively at the possible opportunities for postwar cultural revolution.

Milosz is unwilling, however, to adopt the nihilism of the Spirit of History, whose only relish is for extirpation, whose only claim is that of Necessity. The poet names History "an inferior god to whom time and the fate / Of one-day-long kingdoms is submitted." There are divinities superior to History, and for Milosz these include human memory, freedom, happiness, fidelity, and, not least, mathematics and the universal Forms:

> Plato and his ideas: on the earth hares, foxes, and horses run about and pass on, but somewhere up above the ideas of hareness, foxness, and horseness live on eternally, along with the idea of the triangle and Archimedes' principle, which have not been overturned by chaotic, death-contaminated empirical evidence.[2]

Yet where so many poets have failed either to tell the truth or to find an adequate form, how can anyone succeed? In an eloquent passage that reaches from plainness to sublimity, Milosz asks how a poet is to avoid "two sharp edges"—the Scylla of falsifying idealism and the Charybdis of dismissive rationalism:

> With what word to reach into the future,
> With what word to defend human happiness—
> It has the smell of freshly baked bread—
> If the language of poets cannot search out
> Standards of use to later generations?
> We have not been taught. We do not know at all
> How to unite Freedom and Necessity.
>
> In a dream the mind visits two sharp edges.
> Woe to the unearthly, the radiant ones.
> While storming heaven, they neglect the Earth
> With its joy and warmth and animal strength.
> Woe to the reasonable, the heavy-minded.
> Their lies will extinguish the morning star,
> A gift more durable than Nature is, or Death.

It is thrilling to watch Milosz's maneuvers between the edges, as he veers from the bluntest abstraction—"We do not know at all /

How to unite Freedom and Necessity"—to biblical anathema—
"Woe to the unearthly . . . / Woe to the reasonable." He then moves
on to the morning star, and the symbol of hope is said to be not
(as one might expect) "nobler" or "more sublime" than Nature or
Death, but more "durable" (a word of plain empirical carpenterlike
recommendation). It is at moments like these that one is grateful
for the readableness of Hass's translation: it does not get in the
way; it is transparent; it renders the urgency of these choices for
the Milosz of 1955, weighing his past in the French exile to which
his calling has brought him. The poet's education in Catholicism
had given him a weakness for "the unearthly, the radiant ones";
the practice of diplomacy had exposed him to the claims of "the
reasonable, the heavy-minded." It is characteristic of the poet's lifelong search for a *tertium quid* that he opposes to these two claims
not a third ideology of his own, but an image and an emotion: the
radiant star of hope. In the same way, in representing human happiness, Milosz gives it not a definition but a smell—the morning
fragrance of new-baked bread. In spite of his powerful intellect,
Milosz never forgets that the poet's strength comes from the presence in his language of the senses, the muscles, the fingertips, the
body that is at once corporeal and virtual.

...2...

Part III continues as the war climaxes in the 1944 Warsaw Uprising, an event tersely described by the poet Anna Swir (b. 1909),
who, like Milosz, lived through those days of revulsion and inef-
faceable trauma. She sets the stage, and then moves to the Uprising itself:

> Warsaw was transformed into a wasteland filled with
> corpses, ruins and smouldering ashes. That part of the popu-
> lation which survived the inferno was driven out and deported
> to various concentration camps. After the capitulation, Ger-
> man soldiers systematically burned and dynamited the remain-
> ing buildings. . . .
> Corpses lay about in the streets, and the stench of rotting
> bodies rose from the ruins. Despite these horrible conditions,
> the city put up a heroic struggle for sixty-three days.[3]

In describing the latter part of the war, Milosz adopts the dispassionate manner of a chronicler, recording how young poets fell one after another in untimely and violent deaths:

Copernicus: the statue of a German or a Pole?
Leaving a spray of flowers, Bojarski perished. . . .
Trzebinski, the new Polish Nietzsche,
Had his mouth plastered shut before he died. . . .
Baczynski's head fell against his rifle. . . .
Gajcy, Stronski were raised to the sky,
A red sky, on the shield of an explosion.

American readers, turning to Milosz's notes, will read the histories of some of these poets' deaths, well known to Milosz's Polish readers. I quote a few sentences from the notes to show the rich underpinning of narrative on which Milosz's swift poetic shorthand depends.

For Bojarski, a note on a youthful gesture turning fatal:

A statue of Nicholas Copernicus . . . stands in the center of Warsaw. . . . On May Day in 1943 . . . three poets . . . decided to lay flowers in the national colors at the foot of the monument. It was a students' prank. An exchange of shots with the German police ensued and one of them, Waclaw Bojarski, was mortally wounded.

As for Tadeusz Gajcy (1922–1944), he is considered, together with Baczyński, the most gifted poet among his contemporaries:

In the Warsaw Uprising, together with a friend, the poet Zdzislaw Stroiński (1921–1944), he was in an action in a neighborhood which was the scene of particularly fierce battles. The street changed hands several times. The Germans dug a tunnel, mined the building the poet's unit was defending, and blew it up.

With this roll call of the fallen, *A Treatise on Poetry* begins to seem one repeated death knell for the poets of modern Poland. Those just mentioned were a decade younger than Milosz, but the direct or indirect death toll included many who were older. As one reads

Milosz's notes, the names accumulate: Wladyslaw Sebyla (1902–1940), executed by the Russians at Katyn Woods; Tadeusz Zeleński (1874–1941), executed by the Nazis; Jan Lechoń, a political émigré who committed suicide in New York in 1956; Józef Czechowicz (1903–1939), killed by a German bomb in Lublin; Lucjan Szenwald (1909–1944), killed in an accident while his unit of the Red Army was fighting in Poland. To these Milosz adds, as a group, the young nationalist poets "who were children when the war broke out. . . . [They] perished one by one, in Auschwitz, in street executions, in combat."

The carnage around him gave Milosz's own survival a freakishness that sharpened both his senses and his testimony. It is the sheer weight of facts borne by A Treatise on Poetry that lends the poem its somber coloration. It is an assemblage of reflections, yes; but those reflections are erected on an infernal ground with which the whole world is now familiar, at least from photographs of barricades, gravepits, and crematoria. In a brief characterization of the poetry of his era, Milosz once remarked on that poetry's "mixture of macabre and humorous elements, its preoccupation less with the ego than with dramas of history, [and] the relish with which it handles and remodels moral maxims."[4] Unusual in a peacetime lyric, these become normal features in poems composed at a time when the maxims of received "culture" are exploded and when the poet must try to encompass, by irony and humor as well as by horror, the grotesque and criminal spectacle of war.

• • •

Many of Milosz's notes to A Treatise on Poetry reflect his own wartime and postwar perplexities. "The mysterious link between poetry and politics is complex, difficult to analyze," Milosz writes, "yet its existence was understood by many twentieth-century poets who had analogous experiences in their own countries during these years of war and revolution." And what is this link? "It meant that a mental act, securing a grasp on reality, preceded the poetic act, if the poem, however noble its intention, was not to be mere words."[5] The trouble with most political poetry is that it is self-deluding. Milosz had to refuse to write "the sort of patriotic poetry that appeared in innumerable underground publications."[6] He adds, "The number of patriotic anti-Nazi poems was astronomical. Useful at a given moment, they served the purpose of inciting heroic resistance, but their artistic life was short."[7] They had fallen into the imitation of past styles of both thought and form. It was Milosz's genius to find for the *Treatise* a manner of symphonic complexity, ranging from the dulcet to the catastrophic, from the percussive to the pastoral.

How can Milosz end Part III of his poem? With the replacement of postwar with Communist Poland, the Spirit of History has seemed to conquer. Milosz invents a slavish hymn to the Spirit of History, sung by those who are prepared to succumb to Communist rule as inevitable—but that turned out to be no solution for the defecting poet himself. Leaving the dilemma of history open for the moment, Part III nears its close in coming to the most unrepresentable topic of the war: the extermination of Poland's Jews. In recognition of the Shoah (Milosz adopts that name), Part III exhibits, as it comes toward its close, not a lyric by Milosz himself but a song in tercets, voiced by one of the Jews killed in concentration camps. The condemned singer, who goes from future to past in his song, declares that "only a child of the ghetto could utter the words" that would have purified the soil of Poland; but even had such a poet been born, he was annihilated with the rest:

> When they put a rope around my neck,
> When they choke off my breath with a rope,
> I'll turn around once, and what will I be?

> When they give me an injection of phenol,
> When I walk half a step with phenol in my veins,
> What wisdom of the prophets will enlighten me? . . . .

> Soil of annihilation, soil of hate,
> No word will purify it ever.
> No such poet will be born.

> For even if one had been called, he walked
> Beside us to the last gate, for only
> A child of the ghetto could utter the words.

In confessing that he cannot be, has not the right to be, the poet of the Polish Shoah, Milosz leaves a gaping hole in the *Treatise*, the abyss of the murder of the Jewish population.

And because the writer of the *Treatise* sees his nation's literature in ruins, with its young poets cut off, he winds down the merciless Part III, to the reader's utter surprise, with an elegiac collage of Eliotic fragments—a short song by an anonymous Jewish poet; lines from the nineteenth-century Romantic poet Adam Mickiewicz; and bits of an old Polish Christmas carol rewritten in 1925 by the avant-garde poet Titus Czyzewski (1883–1945). Literature dissolves as Poland dissolves, and, the last we hear of it, it is returning to its roots in the sonic babble of folk song and rustic instruments. "On feast days," says the sophisticated and war-exhausted narrator, "we heard another music," and he summons, through Czyzewski's mediation, a rustic carol which begins:

> Ho la ho la
> Lambs bleat baa baa
> Shepherds run to see
> Come to the stable
> As soon as you're able
> Ho la ho la
> Even Jack with his stutter
> Sings to the Mother
> The Holy Mother
> Ho la

Who could have expected such a verse to serve as the stylistic counterbalance for the obliteration of Warsaw? Yet the poet's manner here resembles that of his famous Blakean "naïve" sequence *The World*, written in 1943 as the pure and ideal opposite of the terrors of devastated Warsaw. Just as Czyzewski's carol returns to the spontanous "first idea" of musical and poetic patterning, so, as the canto closes, the narrator, blankly resting from digging potatoes, lights a cigarette and thinks that since everything else has returned to the primal, he should perhaps be reaching not for a match, but for something more primitive, a "tinder box with flint":

So many things have passed, so many things.
And while no work accomplished helps us,
Titus Czyzewski returns with his Christmas carol.
The double bass used to boom, so he booms.

I rolled a cigarette and licked the paper.
Then a match in the little house of my hand.
And why not a tinder box with flint?
The wind was blowing. I sat on the road at noon,
Thinking and thinking. Beside me, potatoes.

Milosz's poetic is summed up in that last line, as "thinking" sits side by side with "potatoes." The conflagration of Part III comes to a fatigued and stoic end, with a faint "*ho la*" and "*baa baa*" still echoing in the air.

•••

And, finally, "Part IV: Natura: *Pennsylvania, 1948–1949*," with its disturbing opening lines: after the nostalgia, intellectuality, and savagery of Milosz's first three cantos, it was shocking to arrive at Part IV and read the gentle pastoral beginning:

The garden of Nature opens.
The grass at the threshold is green.
And an almond tree begins to bloom.

From an Inferno to a Paradiso. Was this, I wondered, where Milosz would end? Fleeing from history to dwell in the garden of Eden? I should have known better: for all his naturalist's love of the biological world, Milosz knows, looking at Nature in the form of a butterfly, that its colors are "inexpressible, formed elsewhere, hostile to art." Yet, posted as a diplomat to Washington in 1948 and tempted to defect to America, the poet travels to a lake in the woods of northern Pennsylvania to pursue his search for the American beaver, remembered from books of his childhood. It is night, and Milosz is almost invisible; but the beaver, sensing a human presence, dives underwater to conceal himself; and the poet announces regretfully that "my scent in the air, my animal smell, / Spreads, rainbow-like, scares the beaver: / A sudden *splat*." There follows a beautiful suspended moment in which the poet almost becomes the animal self he had longed to behold:

> I remained where I was
> In the high, soft coffer of the night's velvet,
> Mastering what had come to my senses:
> How the four-toed paws worked, how the hair
> Shook off water in the muddy tunnel.

But the poet must return to himself as he acknowledges how the beaver differs from him—it lives without self-consciousness, and he cannot:

> It does not know time, hasn't heard of death,
> ˙Is submitted to me because I know I'll die.

This failed attempt to take on an unself-conscious New World existence presages Milosz's inability to forsake Europe for an apolitical solitude. "I remember everything," he says; he is a citizen not of Nature but of History. Only poetry, he is certain, can preserve the existential detail of history as it was: and history now offers itself to the poet not as a grisly spectre but as a muse. As Keats cried out to Psyche, in his moment of vocation, "Yes, I will be thy priest," so Milosz, in a moment of immense poignancy, summons the first historian, Herodotus, and crystallizes the vow of his calling—to preserve the past in images. He focuses his aim by reaching for the powerful metaphysical image of the plumb line as a symbol of virtue:

> Yes, to gather in an image
> The furriness of the beaver, the smell of rushes,
> And the wrinkles of a hand holding a pitcher
> From which wine trickles. Why cry out
> That a sense of history destroys our substance
> If it, precisely, is offered to our powers,
> A muse of our gray-haired father, Herodotus,
> As our arm and our instrument, though
> It is not easy to use it, to strengthen it
> So that, like a plumb with a pure gold center,
> It will serve again to rescue human beings.

It is hard to refrain from quoting all the sublime moments of Part IV, for example the hymn to America ("America for me has the pelt of a raccoon . . . America's wings are the color of a cardinal") and the ode to October. But I must mention at least the conclusion of the *Treatise*, a passage full of silent tears. Milosz, after all, is unable to shed his past; he sails back to Europe on the churning ocean of Nature, deprived, like Wordsworth, of any consoling mythological vision of Proteus:

> It's not fulfilled: the old hope that Neptune
> Will show his beard, trailing a retinue of nymphs.
> Nothing but ocean which boils and repeats:
> In vain, in vain.

Happiness—epitomized by a verse of Horace learned at school—is not in prospect for this traveller. Horace's mythological tableau of love and music was voiced in liquid words: *Iam Cytherea choros ducit Venus imminente luna*, "Already Cytherean Venus leads choruses, dancing under the rising moon."[8] The poetry that pierced the boy Milosz in secondary school—so much so that he carved it into his wooden school bench, to have it before him always—seems now to represent nothing but an unavailable, or forever lost, sensual and aesthetic utopia. And so, in the desolation of his return to Europe, the poet, recalling the storm winds of war, summarizes the burden of civilization:

> The ship's body, creaking, carries the freight
> Of our foolishness, vagueness, and hidden faith,
> The dirt of our subjectivity, and the homeless
> White faces of the ones who were killed in combat.
> Carries it where? To the isles of bliss? No,
> In us storm winds drowned that stanza of Horace
> A penknife worked into a wooden bench at school.
> It will not find us in this salt and void:

> *Iam Cytherea choros ducit Venus imminente luna*

The Latin line, without a final punctuation mark, ends *A Treatise on Poetry*. The lyric verse, the poet has said, "will not find us": but in our gloomy denial of it we have found it nevertheless. Memory, saturating the very atmosphere of the return journey to Europe, has dredged it up as one of those free-floating unpunctuated fragments shored against "the dirt of our subjectivity" and the drained faces of the war dead. It is no surprise to learn that the Polish translator of *The Waste Land* was the young prewar Milosz.

Milosz's huge and amazing serial meditation, an epic on the conflict of History and Poetry, will find an adequate commentary only from those who can read it in Polish. Yet even in English, *A Treatise on Poetry* seems to me the most comprehensive and moving poem of this half-century. It will be excerpted and anthologized; and its blunt assertions about what poetry must, and must not, attempt will become part of the collective *ars poetica* of our culture.

There exists, still untranslated, an earlier verse-treatise by Milosz, the *Treatise on Morals*, written in Washington in 1948 and described by Milosz as "a poem that mocks socialist realism." It is said to end with "a prediction of coming annihilation."[9] The newly available *Treatise on Poetry* makes one curious about its brother poem and makes one hope that the poet and his steadfast translator may turn it, too, into English.

...3...

Czeslaw Milosz, working energetically still, will be ninety on 30 June 2001. Behind him stretch his millions of written words—poems, novels, essays, a history of Polish literature, lectures, articles, translations, introductions, anthologies, letters, transcribed conversations, and interviews. Milosz has the indomitable strength of the committed writer, urgently pouring out, for the past seventy years, works too numerous, and too complex, to be grasped in their entirety by any single reader's mind. His restless curiosity has led him into far regions of political, religious, literary, and personal acquaintance, some of it memorialized in the curious book just published here under the title *Milosz's ABC's*, vigorously translated by Madeline Levine. Like everything else Milosz has written, it is fascinatingly unpredictable in its sentiments and its assertions. It is an alphabet book, with varying numbers of entries under each letter: for "A" there are twenty-nine entries, for "Z," two. These entries are sometimes playful: under "A" we find not only proper names ("Abramowicz," "Alik") but also "Adam and Eve" and "After All" and "Alcohol." *Milosz's ABC's* is an eclectic collection, and one that must be read not as an encyclopedia but as a journal of memories. In an "Envoi," Milosz explains the nature of the book:

My time, my twentieth century, weighs on me as a host of voices and the faces of people whom I once knew, or heard about, and now they no longer exist. Many were famous for something, they are in the encyclopedias, but more of them have been forgotten, and all they can do is make use of me, the rhythm of my blood, my hand holding the pen, in order to return among the living for a brief moment. . . .

Perhaps my ABC's are instead of: instead of a novel, instead of an essay on the twentieth century, instead of a memoir.

Milosz does not mince words: Simone de Beauvoir is called "a nasty hag"; repelled by the entertainment industry, Milosz says, "Los Angeles horrifies me"; the entry on Rimbaud opens with the reproving sentence "He caused his mother and his entire family a great deal of grief." This unbuttoned quality makes Milosz's ABC's entertaining, if sometimes intemperate.

But the truculent Milosz is not the only Milosz we meet in the ABC's. In his many brief biographies of persons unknown (at least to an American reader), Milosz shows himself a master of the informal sketch, a genre part picture, part biography, part gossip, part obiter dicta, but rarely (given the circumstances of Milosz's life) uninvaded by tragedy. A sample entry on one Mieczyslaw Kotarbiński, a painter, though it begins genially, turns dark:

> Mieczyslaw wanted to help his fellow man, including Jews. For that, he was incarcerated in Pawiak prison and was executed in 1943.

Such sudden reversals of tone, more than any single piece of information, convey Milosz's anguish at the reversals of history, as execution writes the epitaph for friendship. Another such entry on the journalist Witold Hulewicz begins with a joke about his taking a woman on a motorcycle ride ("they would always say the same thing: 'Shake before using'")—and ends, "Arrested in August 1940, he remained in prison until June 12, 1941. An admirer of German poetry and music, the author of a book about Beethoven, he was shot at Palmiry on that day." A lesser writer than Milosz would have suppressed the introductory reminiscence of the indecent joke, but the principal stimulus to Milosz's innovations in poetry came from his resolve to let jokes coexist with martyrdom, irony with pathos, wit with denunciation. Beholding twentieth-century reality, he devised that cinematic montage that we call the Miloszian manner.

•••

In the ABC's, there are interesting mini-essays on writers—Frost, Dostoevsky, Whitman. Those who think of Milosz as a religious writer will find themselves occasionally taken aback: he says of Dostoevsky that "he wrote in a letter to Mrs. Fonvizin that if he were ordered to choose between the truth and Christ, he would choose Christ." Milosz then dryly adds:

> Those who would choose the truth are probably more honorable, even if the truth appears on the surface to deny Christ (as Simone Weil argued). At least they are not relying on their fantasy and not constructing idols in their own image.[10]

Milosz's ABC's should be savored in small doses, not only as a collection of pensées but as a book of historical snapshots. We see the young Milosz, his wife Janka, and his friend the writer Jerzy Andrzejewski producing together, in occupied Warsaw, the first underground chapbook of Milosz's poetry:

> Antoni Bohdziewicz supplied the paper and the duplicating machine, Janka sewed the books, and Jerzy helped out. . . . Janka was very sober-minded and inclined to irony, and she did not care for the Conradian lyricism . . . she saw in Jerzy's work, as she would tell him frankly during our vodka-drinking sessions at the Under the Rooster bar.[11]

But after this companionable glimpse of writers defying perilous odds with conversation and vodka, Milosz's writing slips almost involuntarily into historical elegy, and the tone turns tragic:

> My dearest shades, I cannot invite you to converse with me, for behind us, as only we three know, lies our tragic life. Our conversation would develop into a lament in three voices.[12]

Even here, in the least ironic, most lyric moment of his ABC's, Milosz's analytic objectivity glimmers through, defining his own lyric genre of lament. Every one of his poems, it could be said, is "a lament in three voices"—the personal, the historical, the ironic. He has always stubbornly refused to give up any one of the three; his tempestuous and overwhelming *Treatise* proves the worth of that tenacious resolve.

...NOTES...

1. [Czeslaw Milosz, *A Treatise on Poetry*, translated from the Polish by the author and Robert Hass (New York: Ecco, 2001).]

2. Czeslaw Milosz, *Milosz's ABC's*, translated from the Polish by Madeline Levine (New York: Farrar, Straus and Giroux, 2001), p. 287.

3. *Postwar Polish Poetry*, Third Edition, edited by Czeslaw Milosz (Berkeley: University of California Press, 1983), pp. 70–71.

4. Ibid., p. xii.

5. [Milosz, *Treatise*, pp. 100–101.]

6. [Ibid., p. 101.]

7. [Ibid., p. 103.]

8. [Horace, *Odes*, Book 1, Poem 4.]

9. Ewa Czarnecka and Aleksander Fiut, *Conversations with Czeslaw Milosz*, translated by Richard Lourie (New York: Harcourt Brace Jovanovich, 1987), pp. 142–143.

10. [Milosz, *ABC's*, p. 102.]

11. [Ibid., p. 54. This recollection occurs in Milosz's entry on Balzac.]

12. [Ibid., pp. 54–55.]

At the Border

...JORIE GRAHAM...

I'm not sure a definition of "poetics" is useful, or even possible, for a poet. In the end, I believe most signature styles are born as much out of temperament—and its rare *original* idiosyncracies— as anything else. When I read Beckett's letters, I hear the Beckett of the novels and plays in the most occasional prose—discussing his health or the weather. We might, because of our historically defensive position, which has given rise to much fascinating theory, feel obliged, especially staring into the twin inscrutable faces of barbarism and science, to formulate and defend our temperamental instincts in more programmatic terms, of which "poetics," as a feeling and as a strongly felt notion, is a site.

At any rate, as a possible working rudder, for my own use, I would say I try, in my acts of composition, to experience subjectivity and objectivity at their most frayed and fruitful and morally freighted juncture. I try to do so as "honestly" as I can—as I believe that accurate representation of this juncture is possible, and that character is involved in approaching that border.

Character: good faith; generosity toward the world (when it comes to letting go of some ego, for example); admission of the *sensation* of defeat into the thinking process without having to turn immediately to defensive action (irony, for example); effort; allowing, and then taking responsibility for, ambition; regard for one's elders; admission of the fear of joy; joy; admission of the fear of power; power; and, finally, courage—right there at the core of the act of composition—the courage not to let up on the belief in language; right there at the core, feeling the essential self, not being afraid of being "found out" by philosophy; not using intelligence to protect from that sensation of bedrock unknowing, fundamental empty-handedness.

If there is anything I love most, in the poems I love, it is the audible braiding of that bravery, that essential empty-handedness, and that willingness to be taken by surprise, all in one voice. It is what makes the "human" sound to me. Another soul speaking across the distance—or just the *difference*—to me. And by audible I also mean audible in (or by) the form. I love the sound of what is called "earnestness." I don't experience irony with much natural, instinctive force: it seems a capacity, a world view, drawn by, and driven by, a power model of reality. In ironic perception the speaker, or the perceiver, always wins out over the world. I'm more naturally drawn, in this general arena of experience, to paradox, where the forces are more equal. Best of all, though, I like it when the world "wins" (great acts of description, actions of mind compelled by the poem more than the poet, "cries" of their *occasion*, turns where the turning is a reaction to the world's action). I love it when the occasion is truly reached by the act of imagination, where the perceiving mind, and the imagining restlessness, is, in its language, imprinted, stained by the world, made to take the force of it in (what the miracle of syntax can absorb, encode, reveal, transmit, reenact).

As for the trustworthiness—or even the possibility—of the experience of reality: I often feel like Johnson refuting Berkeley—my toe kicking the stone. The world is there, but the border between the self and the world is, as I see it, a differently fluid juncture according to each person's occasion. I "choose" occasions, therefore, with a mind to keeping the problem—with all its moral, political, spiritual, and aesthetic implications—as alive to me as possible. Shifts in my "style" are a large part of that process.

Finally, I'm not sure I believe that the problem concerning the "limits" of language—or of representation—actually affects us as much as we like to think it does. After many years of assuming that such a philosophical position was utterly natural to my own thinking—and pervasive, obviously, in the thinking of my era—I've come to some private conclusions. However much language and its capacity for representation might—and probably does—have its tortured limits, we find ourselves, as the users of it, less near its border than we might like to imagine, and at no risk of reaching it, however much we all fuss (sometimes quite wonderfully and movingly) over the issue. Such worrying *does*, of course, lend instant high-seriousness to any poetic situation. And knowing of, as well as positing, such limits to language's capacity to represent is an interesting conceptual activity. In practice, though, there's nothing being said, thought, felt, intuited, imagined—or experienced—by the user of language today that seems to me to have reached its limits.

If Shakespeare, Dickinson, and Celan didn't reach that border, we probably needn't worry the issue. In fact, when poets such as these grapple with the edges of utterance, where silence seems the only possible next step for the speaker to undertake, it is not because language has failed the author, it seems to me, but because the human speaker has reached the point where the action of mind *takes place* in silence. Just because emotion—or thought—sometimes grows wordless does not imply that words fail that emotion or thought. It implies that certain textures of experience are by their nature silent. This is an issue that interests and perhaps confuses much contemporary poetry. As far as I can tell, there's really nothing whose *nature* it is to be linguistic (even if not obviously or easily so, even thoughts or feelings that trill at the farthest reaches of the sayable) that can't be ultimately rendered by powerful and accurate uses of language. There are, of course, some things whose nature is *not* linguistic (thoughts that dwell "too deep for tears"). One of the interesting things about poetic art is that it attempts to include those in its body as well.

That capacity to "express" the ineffable, the inexpressible, the emissary of the nonverbal territories of intuition, deep paradox, conflicting bodily impulses as well as profoundly present yet non-languaged spiritual insights, even certain emotional crisis states—these are the wondrous haul that the nets of "deep image," "collective emotive image," haiku image-clusters, musical effects of all kinds (truths only introduced via metrical variation, for example), and the many hinge actions in poems (turns, leaps, associations, lacunae) bring onto the shore of the *made* for us. The astonishments of poetry, for me, reside most vividly in its capacity to make a reader receive utterable and unutterable realities at once.

But where the terrain is linguistic, and the failure linguistic, we may just need to grow more skillful. There again it is perhaps a matter of temperament. The magnificent instrument we call language certainly isn't the problem.

Lux Perpetua
Seamus Heaney's Electric Light

...DENNIS O'DRISCOLL...

In Seamus Heaney's collections, the last shall usually be first. Many critics over the years have observed that the final poem in a Heaney volume will serve advance notice of what may be expected in the collection that follows. Blake Morrison, who—in his 1982 study of the poet—pioneered this prognostic or divinatory approach to the Heaney canon, wrote of *Field Work* (1979) that it begins "not at the beginning but, as is Heaney's custom, with the last poem of the book that preceded it."[1] The critic is not reproving the poet for repetition but admiring Heaney's orderly transfer of power from book to succeeding book, as—in Morrison's own words—he "takes up and develops" the theme of the final poem of the previous collection. *Field Work*—in which the Ulster-born Heaney takes root in the Irish Republic—continues to probe artistic and political dilemmas of the kind which are adumbrated in "Exposure," the closing poem of *North* (1975). In time, the "Ugolino" episode from Dante's *Inferno*, with which *Field Work* ended, would point the way forward to the penitential *purgatorio* of the title sequence of *Station Island* (1984); and the "bare wire" poetry plaited into the "Sweeney Redivivus" sequence, the third and final section of *Station Island*, would lead toward the plain-speaking parables of *The Haw Lantern* (1987). "And so on," as Heaney himself writes in the final line of "The Thimble" in *The Spirit Level* (1996).

"The Thimble" was not the last word in *The Spirit Level*. The collection ended with one of Heaney's most affecting poems, "Post-script," retracing a wind-buffeted drive on Ireland's west coast, a drive in which the light and the foam and the sight of "a flock of swans" (maybe even a Yeatsian "nine-and-fifty" of the birds)[2] left him inwardly as well as outwardly shaken:

> Useless to think you'll park and capture it
> More thoroughly. You are neither here nor there,
> A hurry through which known and strange things pass
> As big soft buffetings come at the car sideways
> And catch the heart off guard and blow it open.

As early as 1979, when he turned forty, Seamus Heaney was expressing concern that, as one gets older, the "space occupied by the instinctual life" contracts. Nearly twenty years later, "Post-script" rejoices not only in the vision of the slate gray lake and foaming ocean, swans, and sky, which he has been momentarily granted but also in the process of inspiration itself, the capacity of an aging heart to still spontaneously respond to the world, to be caught "off guard" and, in an image used irenically and almost ironically by an Ulster poet, blown open. "Postscript" is such a risky poem, so tentative, so contingent, that it would be difficult to ret-rospectively press it into service as offering any tangible clues about Heaney's ensuing collection, *Electric Light* (published five years after *The Spirit Level*), except in the general sense of affirming the poet's determination to keep his imaginative arteries open for the next hoped-for flush of inspiration, the next heartfelt epiphany.

Even if "Postscript" fails to fully conform to the soothsaying theory of Heaney's work, it does find an exact companion piece in the poem "Ballynahinch Lake," included in *Electric Light*. Beginning briskly with "so," the much discussed opening word of Heaney's *Beowulf* translation, a word strongly suggestive of an ongoing nar-rative, the poem is a postscript to "Postscript." The setting again is a lake with "waterbirds" in the west of Ireland but it is no longer "useless to think you'll park and capture" the scene: "this time, yes, it had indeed / Been useful to stop." If the swan-bearing lake of "Postscript" has its literary antecedent in "The Wild Swans at Coole," "Ballynahinch Lake" may owe something to Wordsworth's "uncertain heaven received / Into the bosom of the steady lake."[3]

In neither "Postscript" nor "Ballynahinch Lake," however, does Heaney's respect for his literary elders stifle his own voice; pace, language, and imagery all conspire to reveal his authorship:

So we stopped and parked in the spring-cleaning light
Of Connemara on a Sunday morning
As a captivating brightness held and opened
And the utter mountain mirrored in the lake
Entered us like a wedge knocked sweetly home
Into core timber.

Heaney's acknowledgement of his literary peers and forebears, principally confined to his essays and interviews at first, has increasingly spilled over into his poems through citation, homage, dedication, and elegy. If Yeats and Wordsworth are subtly present in the poems just mentioned, so representative a cross section of the literary and mythological pantheon—including Virgil, Graves, Brodsky, Hopkins, Patrick Kavanagh, and any number of figures from Greek literature and mythology—populates *Electric Light* that Heaney may seem in danger of reaching reflexively for a literary quotation or developing an overdependency on poetical or mythological allusions. While such dangers are real, and Heaney is no doubt sensitive to them, it is bracing to behold a poet—especially one whose vast readership extends far beyond the academy—refusing to pander to lazy populism and, instead, choosing to make ever greater demands on his audience without losing contact with his "instinctual life."

The Latin fragments, Greek and Irish myths, Shakespearean quotations, and *Beowulf* references will perplex admirers of Heaney's early books where an occasional cameo appearance by Undine, Venus, or Narcissus was the only barrier between the reader and uncomplicated lyrical bliss. Yet Heaney is still capable of eidetic lyrical poetry which is as transparent as the "water-roof" through which he spies on the fish in the single-sentence "Perch," a masterpiece of water music in one movement:

Perch on their water-perch hung in the clear Bann River
Near the clay bank in alder-dapple and waver,

Perch we called "grunts," little flood-slubs, runty and ready,
I saw and I see in the river's glorified body

That is passable through, but they're bluntly holding the pass,
Under the water-roof, over the bottom, adoze,

Guzzling the current, against it, all muscle and slur
In the finland of perch, the fenland of alder, on air

That is water, on carpets of Bann stream, on hold
In the everything flows and steady go of the world.

The reader of "Perch," with its fluid syntax and liquid rhythms, its assonance and echo, its gestures toward end-rhymes, its visual puns and vivid use of dialect words, is likely to be swept along with the flow of this apparently simple poem before noting that it, too, contains numerous allusions—to the Bible, Heraclitus, and Hopkins's "Pied Beauty," for example. And yet readers who do not respond to these stimuli will nonetheless be rewarded with a verbally, musically, and imagistically satisfying poem; as with the River Bann itself, they are offered an option on a wade in the shallows or a dunk in the deeper currents, just as the poet himself always seems adept both at walking on water and sounding its depths. Heaney remains, almost uniquely in contemporary poetry, an erudite poet who educates rather than alienates his nonspecialist readers; a poet who is as comfortable with Virgil's *Eclogues* as with a popular song like "The Rose of Mooncoin," who can effortlessly situate Stanley Kubrick's 2001: A *Space Odyssey* and "Bob Cushley with his jennet" within the compass of a single poem.

Heaney's example is an instructive one for the future of poetry in English. Although his books outsell any other living poet in English, he is steadfast and uncompromising in his standards and—in the face of the challenges of literary theory and literary politics—stoutly defends the literary canon as a thriving, evolving force. His version of *Beowulf*, an Anglo-Saxon heroic narrative which even college students of Early English tended to shun, on grounds of tedium, single-handedly revived the fortunes of that poem for scholars as well as a general readership. In doing so, he gave practical expression to forthright remarks about the canon, written in 1991, which form part of his essay "On Poetry and Professing":

Poets are . . . more likely to attest without self-consciousness to the living nature of poetic tradition and to the demotic life of 'the canon.' Nowadays, undergraduates are being taught prematurely to regard the poetic heritage as an oppressive imposition and to suspect it for its latent discriminations in the realm of gender, its privilegings and marginalizations in the realms of class and power. All of this suspicion may be salutary enough when it is exercised by a mind informed by that which it is being taught to suspect, but it is a suspicion which is lamentably destructive of cultural memory when it is induced in minds without any cultural possessions whatever. On the other hand, when a poet quotes from memory or from prejudice or in sheer admiration, 'the canon' is manifested in an educationally meaningful way. To put it simply, I believe that the life of society is better served by a quotation-bore who quotes out of a professional love than by an "unmasking"-bore who subverts out of theory.[4]

Typical of the way in which Heaney educates his audience and avoids confounding a general readership is through subtle illustration or annotation of his more arcane references. Having, in *North*, recollected that "Archimedes thought he could move the world if he could find the right place to position his lever," the Heaney crowbar has always been positioned so as to move (in every sense) the world to the largest possible extent, whether through the leverage of intense short lyrics or long unfolding sequences; increasingly, he has experimented with "loose-weave" poems like "Keeping Going" and "The Flight Path" in *The Spirit Level* and "Out of the Bag," "Known World," and the aptly titled "The Loose Box" in *Electric Light*. "Out of the Bag," for instance, quickly swerves from innocent opening stanzas about the doctor's arrival in the Heaney household, where his mother will again give birth ("All of us came in Doctor Kerlin's bag"), to allusions to the hyperboreans and to the sanctuaries of Asclepius. His description of Doctor Kerlin's eyes as "hyperborean" is immediately glossed with the explanatory "beyond-the-north-wind" blue; readers hitherto unfamiliar with the term "hyperborean" can almost supply it for themselves later in the book when they sense it hovering behind the opening line of "To the Shade of Zbigniew Herbert" ("You were one of those from the back of the north wind"), having en route encountered Heaney himself, on vacation in Greece, indulging his way to becoming enjoyably "hyper, boozed, borean."

Similarly, in "Out of the Bag," the uninitiated reader is put at ease when Heaney refers to the sanctuaries of Asclepius. He explains, through consultations with "*poeta doctus* Peter Levi" and "*poeta doctus* (Robert) Graves," that those sanctuaries were "the equivalent of hospitals / In ancient Greece. Or of shrines like Lourdes"; and he memorably describes his own visits to the site of the temple of Asclepius ("It was midday, mid-May, pre-tourist sunlight") and Lourdes ("Hatless, groggy, shadowing myself")—just as, later in the collection, places like Arcadia and the Castalian Spring are lifted out of myth and quickened into life when his own spirited adventures in these real and resonant locations are described. Indeed, in "Sonnets from Hellas," a living goatherd chanced upon "in the forecourt of the filling station" at Arcadia is described as "subsisting beyond eclogue and translation." Heaney's exposure to the poetry of Zbigniew Herbert and Miroslav Holub, two East Europeans who frequently drew on ancient Greek literature, will have helped to convince him of the continued relevance of mythology; these poets, whom he championed in *The Government of the Tongue* (1988), proved their classical and mythological allusions to be resilient enough to survive censorship and universal enough to survive translation into English.

In his own practice as a translator—of Old English, Old Irish, and classical works—Seamus Heaney has been scrupulously respectful toward the original texts, having learned from his long labor on *Sweeney Astray* (1983) that an "obedient, literal" approach yielded more substantial dividends than an imitation of the skillful but exploitative asset-stripping in which Robert Lowell engaged in *Imitations*. There is nothing reverentially dull or piously po-faced about Heaney's translations, however, and his ability to resurrect and revitalize an ancient text can be witnessed in miniature in "Moling's Gloss," one of the brief poems clustered in *Electric Light* under the title "Ten Glosses" (spontaneous Gaelic poems inscribed in the margins of early monastic manuscripts were termed "glosses"). This four-line poem, dating from the tenth century and rhyming *a-a-b-b*, is attributed to Moling (presumably the saint with whom the protagonist reaches an "uneasy reconciliation" in the closing pages of *Sweeney Astray*). In a literal prose rendition by the scholar Gerard Murphy, it reads: "When I am among my seniors I am proof that games are forbidden; when I am among the wild they think I am younger than they." Responding gamely to the humor of the Gaelic text and retaining its terse musicality (though altering the rhyme scheme), Heaney's poem replenishes the original with a contemporary colloquial "gloss":

> Among my elders, I know better
> And frown on any carry-on;
> Among the brat-pack on the batter
> I'm taken for a younger man.

Colloquial, too, is the translation of "Virgil: Eclogue IX" in *Electric Light* ("watch / The boyo with the horns doesn't go for you") but makes no attempt to enact Virgil in present-day dress. What lends a modern reverberation to this faithfully rendered poem is not so much the register of Heaney's language as Virgil's own political undertones ("An outsider lands and says he has the rights / To our bit of ground") and, above all, the debate—redolent of the quandaries aired in the opening essay of *The Government of the Tongue*—about the efficacy of art in the face of terror ("songs and tunes / Can no more hold out against brute force than doves / When eagles swoop"). In translating "Eclogue IX," Heaney is again assisting his readers: in this case, by providing, for an age in which classical studies have waned, a context in which his two other poems in eclogue form—neither of which lays claim to the status of a translation—may be read. In addition, he is enlarging the modern eclogue tradition to which some of the best twentieth-century poets contributed, including Robert Hass, Heaney's fellow Ulsterman Louis MacNeice, and the doomed Hungarian poet Miklós Radnóti. Radnóti, in fact, began work on his devastating poems in eclogue form after he had translated the same Virgil eclogue as Heaney (IX), finding it no doubt similarly capable of acting as a personal and political echo chamber. Heaney himself has tellingly written of Virgil's *Eclogues*: "What these poems prove is that literariness as such is not an abdication from the truth. The literary is one of the methods human beings have devised for getting at reality . . . "

"Glanmore Eclogue," a light, playful poem, set in a part of County Wicklow about which Heaney has been writing since *Field Work*, acknowledges the potential gap between modern poet and wary contemporary reader. A farmer figure, Myles, urges the poet to offer "words that the rest of us / Can understand." This eclogue is essentially a tribute to Ann Saddlemyer, called "Augusta" in the poem—after Lady Gregory whose plays she edited. Saddlemyer, who owned Glanmore Cottage, is termed (in a Yeatsian epigraph to "Glanmore Sonnets," which again tacitly acknowledges the parallel with Lady Gregory) the Heaney family's "heartiest welcomer" to Wicklow; she is best known as a Synge scholar (the playwright— assigned the Virgilian name, Meliboeus, in this eclogue—had close family ties with Glanmore). "Glanmore Eclogue" also portrays a Southern Ireland in which the small farmers who regained their "bit of ground" politically are being "priced out of the market" economically in the Celtic Tiger conditions that prevailed in the 1990s. Like Virgil, Heaney has a firsthand knowledge of farming; the "cows in clover" of "Eclogue IX," with "canted teats / And tightening udders," are the same breed as the County Derry herd which appears in the richly maternal and indeed mammarial final stanza of "Bann Valley Eclogue"—the most impressive of the three eclogues in the collection—set in a land of milk and honey-tinted hay:

> Child on the way, it won't be long until
> You land among us. Your mother's showing signs,
> Out for her sunset walk among big round bales.
> Planet earth like a teething ring suspended
> Hangs by its world-chain. Your pram waits in the corner.
> Cows are let out. They're sluicing the milk-house floor.

The epigraph to "Bann Valley Eclogue," "*Sicelides Musae, paulo maiora canamus*"("Sicilian Muses, sing we greater things" in Sir John Beaumont's enduring version), is the first line of Virgil's "Golden Age" or "Messianic" eclogue, Number IV. "Bann Valley Eclogue" is not so much a parallel translation as an independent text, which is aware of—without being dependent on—the trajectory of Virgil's poem. If Heaney yields to hopes of a golden age for the child whose birth is anticipated in his eclogue, it is because she is being born into a post-cease-fire Ulster; and if the poem predicts an auspicious event, it is certainly not the arrival of a male Messiah. Virgil's expectations of a male birth contrast with Heaney's certainty that the young woman in the poem is bearing a daughter; the baby's father is unmentioned and, in fact, the only identifiable male presence—aside from Virgil—is Heaney himself remembering (through a skein of exhaustively exact adjectives) the shamrock "with its twining, binding, creepery, tough, thin roots" which he picked for his own mother on St. Patrick's Day.

An eclogue can be a miniature drama, and Seamus Heaney has long shown an interest in pitching voice against line, meter against speech: in a radio verse-play (Munro), a version of Sophocles's *Philoctetes* (*The Cure at Troy*), and the dramatic monologues in parts of *Station Island*. One of the most enjoyable and entertaining poems in *Electric Light* is "The Real Names"—a drama in ten brief scenes. The setting is St. Columb's College in Derry, ca. 1954; the dramatis personae are Seamus Heaney and his classmates. Shakespeare, though, is the real hero of the poem: his language has engraved itself deeply into Heaney's memory; and school performances of his dramas (in which—true to Elizabethan practice—female parts were played by boys) are fondly and humorously recollected. As an Irish poet from the nationalist tradition, Heaney has no wish to speak the Queen's English ("My passport's green. / No glass of ours was ever raised / To toast The Queen"); but he is proud to speak Shakespeare's tongue. It takes only the merest whisper from the inner prompter—whether the name of a character from *The Tempest*, a line or two from *The Merchant of Venice*, or an image from *Henry IV Part I*—to transport him to that oak-beamed corner of his memory where an instant chain reaction of Shakespearean associations is set in motion. The most virtuosic cadenza in the poem is an offshoot of a line from *Hamlet*:

> There is a willow grows aslant the brook[5]
> But in the beginning it was *sally tree*.
> Sallies in hedges and sallies on the bank
> Of the Moyola River and black sallies
> Like a line of daunted stragglers bogging down

In the sedge and glarry wetness of our meadow.
The one in the yard was tetter-barked and hollow,
Two-timing earth and air: corona top
Of flick-and-shimmer, sprout-and-tremble growth . . .

One of Seamus Heaney's favorite poems by Robert Lowell, "Epilogue," pleads for "each figure in the photograph" to be accorded "his living name." "The Real Names" not only reveals the identities of those who participated with Heaney in school productions but also lays considerable stress on local habitations and local names—in this instance, Hamlet's willow at Elsinore is supplanted by Heaney's sally at the Moyola River in County Derry. "Sally" is a regional variant on sallow (from the Latin, *salix*, for willow). One is reminded of Heaney's "Mossbawn" essay, in which he remarks of Keats's "Ode to Autumn": "I had a vague satisfaction from 'the small gnats mourn / Among the river sallows,' which would have been complete if it had been 'midges' mourning among the 'sallies.'"[6]

This localizing tendency—already seen in the substitution of Heaney's Glanmore and Bann Valley for Virgil's Arcadia—resurfaces in "On His Work in the English Tongue," a poem in celebration and commemoration of Ted Hughes. As an elegy for a close friend (albeit a fellow writer), this is an intensely literary poem. Even here, however, in the surge of a breathtakingly bravura description of the underside of a bridge ("the tremor-drip / And cranial acoustic of the stone"), Heaney specifies that the structure—which the reader might otherwise have assumed to be a generic bridge or perhaps a bridge in Ted Hughes's Yorkshire—is in fact "the one / Over the railway lines at Anahorish" in County Derry. Seamus Deane has termed Heaney's insistence on the local a species of "domestication . . . a search for an origin." No wonder Heaney has quoted Carson McCullers to the effect that "to know who you are, you have to have a place to come from" and has cited Patrick Kavanagh as illustrative of the fact that "Loved places are important places, and the right names 'snatch out of time the passionate transitory.'" Exotic ground on the road to Piedras Blancas in Spain is compared with the "home ground, / The Gaeltacht, say, in the nineteen-fifties." "The Gaeltacht" (the title refers to one of the Gaelic-speaking districts of Ireland), a yearning poem comprising a roll call of friends from student days, is Heaney's "imitation" of Dante's sonnet to Guido Cavalcanti. And the Gaelic language is again a "domesticating" medium in "Desfina" (one of the "Sonnets from Hellas") where numerous and humorous Gaelic equivalents for Mount Parnassus spill out over dinner with the ouzo:

> Mount Parnassus placid on the skyline:
> Slieve na mBard, Knock Filiocht, Ben Duan.
> We gaelicized new names for Poetry Hill
> As we wolfed down horta, tarama and houmos
> At sunset in the farmyard, drinking ouzos . . .

"Known World," a crucial poem—improvised in form and innovative in theme—demonstrates how important feelings of empathy are for Heaney when he is faced with foreign settings. In the poem, he draws vivid comparisons between Belgrade in the Balkans and Belmullet in Ireland ("Belmullet elders in the streets. / Black shawls, straight walk, the weather eye, the beads"). It is with the empathetic solidarity of a farmer's son that he writes of the rural people displaced by the Kosovan conflict (the poem is dated May 1998), simultaneously viewing them through the "cloud-boil of a camera lens" and the lens of memory:

> At the still centre of the cardinal points
> The flypaper hung from our kitchen ceiling,
> Honey-strip and death-trap, a barley-sugar twist
> Of glut and loathing . . .
> In a nineteen-fifties
> Of iron stoves and kin groups still in place,
> Congregations blackening the length
> And breadth of summer roads.
> And now the refugees
> Come loaded on tractor mudguards and farm carts,
> On trailers, ruck-shifters, box-barrows, prams,
> On sticks, on crutches, on each other's shoulders . . .

The allusion to T. S. Eliot's "Burnt Norton" in those lines is not the only literary reference in "Known World." In fact, much of the poem centers on Heaney's recollections of the companionably bibulous Struga Poetry Festival in Macedonia in 1978 when "we hardly ever sobered." Heaney, always mindful of the dangers of exploiting the sufferings of others ("'punting along' on other people's weeping wounds"), places his images of suffering in the context of his firsthand memories of visiting the Balkan region. Exactly as in *Field Work*, when Ulster violence was at issue ("How culpable was he / That last night when he broke / Our tribe's complicity?"), he prefers to raise pertinent questions than to make presumptuous assertions: "who's to know / How to read sorrow rightly, or at all?" The vignettes of the Struga Festival recreate the giddy exuberance of the occasion—the banter, the booze, the camaraderie—with a wry immediacy. In fact, some of the memories of people (Hans Magnus Enzensberger in panama hat and "pressed-to-a-T cream linen suit") and events (including a sensuously sketched Madonna's Day gathering in the mountains) owe part of their freshness to their origins in contemporaneous notes:

> Then, the notebook says,
> 'People on the move, field full of folk,
> Packhorses with panniers, uphill push
> Of families, unending pilgrim stream.
> Today is workers' day in memory
> Of General Strike. Also Greek Orthodox
> Madonna's Day.'

This reliance on raw notes is not a feature unique to "Known World." One of the previous high points of Heaney's work, the final section of "The Flight Path" in *The Spirit Level*, ends: "Eleven in the morning. I made a note: / 'Rock-lover, loner, sky-sentry, all hail!' / And somewhere the dove rose. And kept on rising." *Field Work*—written when his entrancement with Robert Lowell was at its height—contains a poem, "High Summer," in which lines are quoted from a notebook or letter. Among the features which lend particular significance to "Known World" in the evolution of Seamus Heaney's work are the daring admixture of its registers and the unprecedented heterogeneity of its component sections. It is as if the poet were insouciantly exploring a new poetry path, still demonstrating a willingness to risk fresh directions and at last admitting into his work, albeit self-deprecatingly, the experiences of the international literary traveler (which, at this post-Nobel juncture, it would be dishonest to exclude).

The international literary life features also—but less centrally—in a poem in memory of Joseph Brodsky, "Audenesque." This poem, one of a number of elegies grouped together in the second part of *Electric Light*, is an instance of what Heaney himself has classified as "the Lycidas syndrome" whereby "one artist's sense of vocation and purpose is sent into crisis by the untimely death of another." We are allowed backstage at a reading in western Massachusetts, where Brodsky is decanting pepper vodka, and are taken on board a train in Finland ("Lenin's train-trip in reverse") where Brodsky and Heaney are "swapping manuscripts and quips." Heaney's imitative ingenuity in "Audenesque" is both formal and linguistic: formal in its borrowings from "Wystan Auden's metric feet," the trochaic tetrameter employed in the third section of "In Memory of W. B. Yeats"; linguistic in the way it affectionately and accurately captures the clumsiness of Brodsky's English verse. In a *New York Times Book Review* tribute to Brodsky, Heaney commented on Brodsky's "bewilderment at the self-delusion of second raters" in poetry. But for many of us not privileged to have enjoyed the friendship of this courageous and charismatic man, Brodsky's own first-rateness was a matter for conjecture or for trust, as the "more-than-enoughness" which Heaney associates with true poetry veered toward a kind of "over-the-topness." In Heaney's mimetic virtuosity, we glimpse Brodsky's gauche verbosity:

> Nevermore that wild speed-read,
> Nevermore your tilted head
> Like a deck where mind took off
> With a mind-flash and a laugh,
>
> Nevermore that rush to pun
> Or to hurry through all yon
> Jammed enjambements piling up
> As you went above the top,
>
> Nose in air, foot to the floor,
> Revving English like a car . . .

The appropriateness of "In Memory of W. B. Yeats" as a model for an elegy of Joseph Brodsky lies not only in Brodsky's lifelong obsession with Auden and his devotion to this elegy for Yeats, but also in the fact that both Yeats and Brodsky died on the same "double-crossed and death-marched date, / January twenty-eight." It was during his enforced exile (as a so-called "social parasite") in the Arkhangelsk region of northern Russia that Brodsky wrote his "Verses on the Death of T. S. Eliot," modeled on Auden's elegy.

The finest of the literary elegies clustered in the second part of *Electric Light* is "'Would They Had Stay'd,'" a lament for a quartet of recent Scottish poets which takes its title from Shakespeare's "Scottish play." In approaching his task, Heaney will have been conscious of the majestic precedent set by "Lament for the Makaris," William Dunbar's elegy which he first encountered as a student and which, having modernized the late medieval Scottish text, he recorded for Harvard University's Poetry Room. The four poets lamented by Heaney are Norman MacCaig, George Mackay Brown, the Gaelic-language Somhairle MacGill-Eain (under his more familiar English name, Sorley MacLean), and the bilingual Iain Crichton Smith (under his less familiar Gaelic name, Iain MacGabhainn). The poem contains heroic and heraldic language, worthy of a medieval poem, as well as some interlinked images of deer whose presence in the five sections of the poem is the golden thread which binds this elegy together:

> The color of meadow hay, with its meadow-sweet
> And liver-spotted dock leaves, they were there
> Before we noticed them, all eyes and evening,
> Up to their necks in the meadow.

Not all of the elegies concern literary figures—the deeply touching "Seeing the Sick," for example, elegizes the poet's father. Although his father was an unliterary man and (as commemorated in "The Stone Verdict") a taciturn one, Heaney looks to his own literary forefather, Gerard Manley Hopkins, for an elegiac template with which he can feel comfortable—perhaps because it would have been out of character, embarrassing even, for son to address father directly in matters involving the emotions and affections. Hopkins's elegy for a "big-boned and hardy-handsome" blacksmith facilitates Heaney's oblique and clipped, but intense and unfeigned, tribute to his cattle-dealing father. The poem's title, its opening phrase ("anointed and all"), and much of its imagery derive from Hopkins's "Felix Randal"; both Heaney and Hopkins use the word "tendered" differently (Hopkins in connection with Holy Communion, Heaney with the more secular balm of morphine) but with an equal upwelling of tendresse. The literary imagery illuminates the human portrait and no more occludes the dying father than the allusions to Chaucer, Shakespeare, Dante, and Larkin obliterate the "desperate" grandmother in the poem "Electric Light." The sibylline grandmother's "urgent, sibilant / Ails" excavates a channel for the poet into England, the English language, and great English literature. Again, Heaney shows himself to be a poet so attuned to every verbal nuance that a single word can detonate the history of an entire language:

> We were both desperate

> The night I was left to stay, when I wept and wept
> Under the clothes, under the waste of light
> Left turned on in the bedroom. 'What ails you, child,

> What ails you, for God's sake?' Urgent, sibilant
> Ails, far off and old. Scarcesome cavern waters
> Lapping a boatslip. Her helplessness no help.

> ★

> Lisp and relapse. Eddy of sybilline English.
> Splashes between a ship and dock, to which,
> Animula, I would come alive in time

> As ferries churned and turned down Belfast Lough
> Towards the brow-to-glass transport of a morning train,
> The very 'there-you-are-and-where-are-you?'

> Of poetry itself. Backs of houses
> Like the back of hers, meat-safes and mangles
> In the railway-facing yards of fleeting England,

> An allotment scarecrow among patted rigs,
> Then a town-edge soccer pitch, the groin of distance,
> Fields of grain like the Field of the Cloth of Gold.

To Southwark too I came,
From tube-mouth into sunlight,
Moyola-breath by Thames's 'straunge stronde'.

His grandmother's use of "ails" deepened the child's sense of homesickness because it was at variance with the usage in his own Mossbawn household (where—as the prose poem "Hedge-School" reveals—"What are you crying about now, son?" would be more typical)—early evidence of the future poet's ultrasensitivity to language! The proximity of "ails" to "nails" acts as a mnemonic for Heaney whose abiding memory of his grandmother is of her "smashed thumb-nail." Perhaps the further proximity of "nail" to "alien" is not accidental either, in a poem which opens with his alienation in the strange life and light of his grandmother's house; and the electric light there, to which he was unaccustomed at the time, is now transformed into the *lux perpetua* of poetry as the poem comes to rest on an elegiac note "among beads and vertebrae in the Derry ground."

Seamus Heaney's words have never been mere ciphers, tools which simply record events and reorder experiences. As a devoted exponent of Eliot's "auditory imagination,"[7] words for Heaney are sounds before they are sense or, rather, their sounds are inextricably linked to their sense. By *Wintering Out* (1972), he had begun making language his subject as well as his medium. Just as people's names are sometimes said to contain their destinies, Heaney's place-names contain their topography ("*Anahorish*, soft gradient / of consonant, vowel-meadow"). In *Electric Light*, "ails" is not the only troubling word Heaney has borne with him across the years; as a boarder at St. Columb's College, he was "left . . . winded" by the ominous power packed into the word "attack" which he heard in connection with the Border Campaign in Ulster in 1956.

While poets should, by virtue of their chosen vocation, be virtuosi in the use of language, what most of them actually display is a talent—as unremarkable as it is unrelenting—for mediocre writing; in attempting to distract the reader from their shortcomings, they rely on a panoply of diversionary tactics, from vainglorious obscurity to sensational subject matter. The qualities which, by contrast, make Heaney so deservedly admired include the ability to link evocative words never before found in combination and, indeed, seldom chanced upon in splendid isolation. His ease with words of multiple provenance, from the Gaelic and Anglo-Saxon to the Scots Ulster and Latin; his rooted sense of language as a living dialect; his brio and bravura when it comes to deploying word and trope—these gifts are at the heart of his achievement. There is a radiance about his poems which is an attribute not of his optimism (though it is true that he is more comfortable with celebration than censure) but of the unique space occupied by poems in which the language is revivified and refreshed, renewed and refurbished.

In the satisfyingly loose sequence, "The Loose Box," the section which deals with grain threshing is itself like a machine which picks up momentum incrementally, line by line. Soon, however, it has hummed into life and is generating words "hard as shot" (to borrow a phrase from Heaney's early threshing poem, "The Wife's Tale") as Heaney recalls, and excels, the threshing scene in *Tess of the D'Urbervilles*:

> Raving machinery,
> The thresher bucking sky, rut-shuddery,
> A headless Trojan horse expelling straw
> From where the head should be, the underjaws
> Like staircases set champing—it hummed and slugged
> While the big sag and slew of the canvas belt
> That would cut your head off if you didn't watch
> Flowed from the flywheel. And comes flowing back,
> The whole mote-sweaty havoc and mania
> Of threshing day, the feeders up on top
> Like pyre-high Aztec priests gutting forked sheaves
> And paying them ungirded to the drum.
> Slack of gulped straw, the belly-taut of seedbags.
> And in the stilly night, chaff piled in ridges,
> Earth raw where the four wheels rocked and battled.

This is high-octane writing of a high order, aided by Heaney's verbal compounds ("rut-shuddery," "mote-sweaty," "sag and slew") and abetted by his genius at transmuting observation and experience into language of great physical precision. A comparable moment of mechanical power in poetry occurs in Ted Hughes's winter poem, "Tractor," when the frozen machine, finally coaxed into starting, begins "shuddering itself full of heat." Characteristically, the Hughes poem is more hit-and-miss than Heaney's; while it contains impressively vigorous language, phrases like "a more-than-usually-complete materialization" and "bursting with superhuman well-being and abandon" leave the tractor rusting in anomalous abstractions rather than gearing up for dynamic action. Heaney's tonal and emotional range in *Electric Light* is evident when "The Loose Box" is contrasted with "The Clothes Shrine," a gentle poem—transparent in language and subject matter—which revels in electric light of a less literal kind than the book's title poem. It recalls the "early years" of marriage to his wife, Marie, and is a perfect instance of Heaney's contention that, through "poetic technique," an intimate experience can mutate into "an object to be inspected. It calls you close and the intimacy is not embarrassing":

> It was a whole new sweetness
> In the early days to find
> Light white muslin blouses
> On a see-through nylon line
> Drip-drying in the bathroom
> Or a nylon slip in the shine
> Of its own electricity . . .

The award of the Nobel Prize for Literature in 1995, with all the immense freight of disruption and distraction that accompanied it, has not deflected Heaney from his path as a poet who—however allusive and erudite his work may have grown over the years—is drawn to the primal truths at the heart of the everyday. His appetite for poetry and his relish for language are unabated in this post-Nobel collection; individual lines (such as his description of flower seed packets as "sifting lightness and small jittery promise") and individual poems (such as "The Little Canticles of Asturias"— a bonsai *Divine Comedy*, right down to its final "*stela*"), throughout *Electric Light*, belie the view that poetry can speak to our times only if it is constantly questioning and ironizing its own procedures. His self-questioning tends to be ethically rather than theoretically motivated and, even if we accept that the limits of one's language mark the limits of one's world, Seamus Heaney's language seems so unimpeded, so undaunted, that what his poetry ultimately conveys is a sense of the limitless possibilities of the art in the hands of the truly gifted.

Having earlier, and with some hesitation, applied to "Postscript" (the last poem in The Spirit Level) Blake Morrison's theory that the final poem of a Heaney collection yields clues to the subsequent collection, I would like to add a postscript of my own. "Postscript" is a poem which, taking a cue from its title, the reader may consider separately from the preceding poems in The Spirit Level; there is a case, therefore, for contending that it falls to "Tollund," the penultimate poem in that 1996 collection, to illuminate the reader forward into Electric Light. Set in Denmark at the time of the 1994 IRA cease-fire announcement, the poem marks Heaney's first visit to the rural setting of "The Tollund Man," a "bog poem" recognized as central to Heaney's output since its appearance in Wintering Out. At the time of writing "The Tollund Man," the analogy which was foremost in Heaney's mind was between the Iron Age man (who had been excavated from a Jutland bog)—apparently the sacrificial victim of a violent ritual—and the violence which was rampant in Ulster:

> Out there in Jutland
> In the old man-killing parishes
> I will feel lost,
> Unhappy and at home.

By the time, over twenty years later, "Tollund" came to be written, "things had moved on." The poet (who, typically, invokes some Ulster place-names—"It could have been Mulhollandstown or Scribe") is becoming found, happy and at home:

> . . . it was user-friendly outback
> Where we stood footloose, at home beyond the tribe,
>
> More scouts than strangers, ghosts who'd walked abroad
> Unfazed by light, to make a new beginning
> And make a go of it, alive and sinning,
> Ourselves again, free-willed again, not bad.

Heaney's weighing of his "responsible *tristia*" reached a peak in the "Station Island" sequence; but, after its somber processions and cathartic professions, convincingly and movingly realized, he finally began to heed the exhortations of James Joyce's ghost to "write / for the joy of it," to "let others wear the sackcloth and the ashes. / Let go, let fly, forget." Heaney remains a profoundly responsible poet, incapable of ever forgetting the overriding fidelity of the artist to the truth he or she experiences; at the same time, his capacity to "credit marvels," never in doubt, has found a fresh impetus in the wake of the fragile peace process celebrated in "Tollund." Admittedly, poems like "The Border Campaign" and "Known World" show Heaney continuing to engage with political subject matter; and "The Augean Stables," one of the "Sonnets from Hellas," chillingly records a moment when the "whitewashed light" of Greece was clouded by news of the sectarian murder of a friend in Ulster. The fact that the friend, Sean Brown, was an athlete (a member, as Heaney himself had been, of the Gaelic Athletic Association or GAA) confers a particular poignancy on the location of the poem in Olympia:

> And it was there in Olympia, down among green willows,
> The lustral wash and run of river shallows,
> That we heard of Sean Brown's murder in the grounds
> Of Bellaghy GAA Club. And imagined
> Hose-water smashing hard back off the asphalt
> In the car park where his athlete's blood ran cold.

Despite the eclogues and other excursions into the pastoral, therefore, death (whether violent or natural) weighs heavily on parts of *Electric Light*. Nonetheless, the "light" emphasized by Heaney's title animates many of these post-cease-fire poems and there is a "Tollund"-like lightness to his poetical gait in the mischievous way, for instance, he plays with a title like "Red, White and Blue." In previous collections such a title would, in all likelihood, have presaged a politically tinctured poem. Here, the poem's colors are fondly associated with items of clothing worn by Marie during their courtship and the early years of their marriage. The "hunting-jacket look" of the scarlet coat in the first of the poem's three sections does not prompt references to Yeats's Anglo-Irish world of "hard-riding country gentlemen" any more than the knights and battlements of "Castle Childbirth" are used, in the second section, to make a point about foreign conquerors. When, in the third part, the young couple hitchhiking in the Irish Republic in 1963 are drawn into a sensitive political discussion, they plead, "We're from the north." Heaney, in this song of innocence, clearly relishes the halcyon memory of a pre-"Troubles" interlude when to be from the north was to be from a place which (discriminatory though it was for Catholics) was not yet synonymous with violence.

Although a slighter poem than "Red, White and Blue," "Turpin Song" too is notable for its relaxed approach toward potentially political imagery, and its free associations culminate in a gesture from the film 2001: A Space Odyssey rather than a metaphor for the "Troubles." What makes the poem memorable is its photographically exact evocation of an antique pistol, displayed at home during the late forties:

> The horse pistol, we called it:
> Brass inlay smooth in the stock,
> Two hammers cocked like lugs,
> Two mottled metal barrels,
> Sooty nostrilled, levelled.

Twenty years before the onset of the modern "Troubles," any fear tainting this pistol in the poet's childhood is likely to have been due to parental chastisement for having "transgressed" and left the firearm for dead ("it lies there, broken in bits"). And one wonders if this gunslinging child might be father to the celebrated poet of "Digging" with his "snug as a gun" pen.

Another possible parallel between The Spirit Level and Electric Light lies in their respective opening poems, "The Rain Stick" and "At Toomebridge." "The Rain Stick" is an opening movement that calls for an encore ("Listen now again"); it makes no apology for a second coming—or a thousandth—to familiar Heaney places and themes: "What happens next / Is undiminished for having happened once, / Twice, ten, a thousand times before." In this spirit, "At Toomebridge" recapitulates earlier Heaney poems (including "A Lough Neagh Sequence" in Door Into the Dark, "Toome" in Wintering Out, and "The Toome Road" in Field Work). Acting as a kind of "You Are Here" sign for Heaney, the poem anchors him firmly at the start of this peripatetic collection in a known and loved place—a place at which a troubled history ("Where the checkpoint used to be. / Where the rebel boy was hanged in '98") is counter-pointed by the "continuous present" of the Bann River and where even "negative ions in the open air / Are poetry to me." A poem almost as short and cryptic as a "gloss," "At Toomebridge" antic-ipates that same seamless weave of time which occurs elsewhere in the collection ("All that was written / And to come I was a part of then") and might be echoing "The Rain Stick," as well as repris-ing the eel imagery of "A Lough Neagh Sequence," when it ends: "As once before / The slime and silver of the fattened eel."

Demonstrating his own version of the "continuous present," Heaney breaks old ground in new ways, relating everything he expe-riences in the wider world to the "known world" of Ulster. Like his exemplar, Patrick Kavanagh, he is aware that to get to know one small field takes a lifetime's exploration. Yet, however distant he may have grown, through time and travel, from the first field— perhaps the "field behind the house" where he was lost among the pea drills as a child—it remains a real place to which he is imaginatively bound and permanently rooted: a touchstone for authenticity and a fertile source of vision. As he writes in "The Loose Box," in lines which again carry a faint echo of Shakespeare ("Now would I give a thousand furlongs of sea for an acre of bar-ren ground: long heath, broom, furze, anything"):[8]

> On an old recording Patrick Kavanagh states
> That there's health and worth in any talk about
> The properties of land. Sandy, glarry,
> Mossy, heavy, cold, the actual soil
> Almost doesn't matter; the main thing is
> An inner restitution, a purchase come by
> By pacing it in words that make you feel
> You've found your feet in what 'surefooted' means
> And in the ground of your own understanding . . .

A book of present and past, multiple births and manifold deaths, of instinctive evocations and intellectual allusions, of the lambently local and the urbanely international, *Electric Light* shows Heaney—

now in his sixties—still eluding categorization, still shirking a "last definition." To paraphrase "A Norman Simile" (one of the "Ten Glosses"), he is marvelously himself; and the poems in this collection—in the punning words which conclude "The Clothes Shrine"—are "got through / As usual, brilliantly." A further "gloss" which it is apposite to quote is "The Bridge": remove the title and you are left with a riddle; remove the bridge and you are looking at the poet himself:

> Steady under strain and strong through tension,
> Its feet on both sides but in neither camp,
> It stands its ground, a span of pure attention,
> A holding action, the arches and the ramp
> Steady under strain and strong through tension.

...NOTES...

1. [Blake Morrison, *Seamus Heaney* (New York: Methuen, 1982), p. 70.]

2. [See Yeats's "The Wild Swans at Coole," line 6.]

3. [See Wordsworth's "There was a Boy, ye knew him well, ye Cliffs" in the 1800 edition of *Lyrical Ballads*. The poem is later incorporated into the 1805 edition of *The Prelude* (Book 5). See *The Fourteen-Book Prelude* by *William Wordsworth*, edited by W. J. B. Owen (Ithaca, N.Y.: Cornell University Press, 1985), pp. 103–104.]

4. [Seamus Heaney, "On Poetry and Professing," in his *Finders Keepers: Selected Prose 1971–2001* (New York: Farrar, Straus and Giroux, 2002), p. 76.]

5. [See 4.7.165 in *Hamlet*, edited by Harold Jenkins, The Arden Shakespeare (New York: Methuen, 1982), p. 373.]

6. [Seamus Heaney, "Mossbawn," *Finders Keepers*, p. 13.]

7. [See the chapter on Matthew Arnold in Eliot's *The Use of Poetry and the Use of Criticism: Studies in the Relation of Criticism to Poetry in England* (Cambridge, Mass.: Harvard University Press, 1933), p. 111: "What I call the 'auditory imagination' is the feeling for syllable and rhythm, penetrating far below the conscious levels of thought and feeling, invigorating every word; sinking to the most primitive and forgotten, returning to the origin and bringing something back, seeking the beginning and the end."]

8. [See 1.1.65–67 in *The Tempest*, edited by Virginia Mason Vaughan and Alden T. Vaughan, The Arden Shakespeare (London: Thomson Learning, 1999).]

Green, Prickly Humanity
Rural Wisconsin's
Exhilarating Lost Poet

...KAREN VOLKMAN...

In the introduction to the new collection of Lorine Niedecker's
works, editor Jenny Penberthy states that the book's ambition is
to establish Niedecker's rightful place in twentieth-century American poetry. Niedecker's problematic publication history, rife with
delays and disappointments, and a personal life that kept her iso-
lated in rural Wisconsin (far from the metropolitan centers so
crucial to the work of the Objectivist poets with whom she is commonly grouped) have conspired to make her a strangely margin-
alized figure. No small part of this strangeness is the beauty of her
wry, precise, often exhilarating work; far from the writings of a
hermetic recluse, Niedecker's lines are full of calls, invitations,
addresses, a poetry of connection soliciting its responsive, articulate other. Penberthy's volume seeks to give full scope to this restless imagination, presenting poems as sequenced in Niedecker's
manuscripts before the truncations and regroupings of actual published volumes, as well as including her radio plays, short prose,
and sequences of uncollected poems from different periods in the
poet's long writing life.

In terms both of circumscribed geography and thwarted dis-
semination of her writing, the obvious analogy is with Dickinson.
Born on 12 May 1903, Niedecker spent little time outside the Wisconsin marshland of Black Hawk Island where she grew up and,
after a year at Beloit College, returned to care for an invalid mother.

Like Dickinson's New England, this landscape becomes almost a collusive subject within the poems, with its birds, fishes, trees, and talking waters. And as Dickinson used hymn structures to provide a communal cadence to her very personal idiom, Niedecker in much of her work echoes folk speech and rhythms to anchor her odd acuity in very short, mostly untitled poems. Emphatically unlike Dickinson, however, she struggled with financial burdens until late in life, working as a proofreader, researcher, and hospital room cleaner while desperately trying to maintain the land and houses inherited after her father's death. Her relationship to nature is intimate and verbal, ranging from rapture to despair to exasperation:

What cause have you
to run my wreathed
rose words
off

you weed
you pea-blossom weed
in a folk
field[1]

As Penberthy points out, Niedecker's wide reading and avid ear attuned her to a range of language use, from historical documents and literary letters to overheard conversations, matter she readily recast in the poems' diverse voicings. Early poems show her interest in dreams and the unconscious, irrational connectives, and multiple planes of perception, as in the three-columned "Canvass." Linking these early writings and her mature work is a persistent investment in what might be called the sound of sense. Her first published poem, "When Ecstasy Is Inconvenient" (grouped by *Poetry* editor Harriet Monroe with "Promise of Brilliant Funeral" and given the dubious title "SPIRALS"),[2] already rings with slant aphorism: "say the time of moon is not right for escape." An affection for the blunt speech of brute common sense often gives her poems the plain poise of wisdom literature, lanced with slides and swerves that leap from her alert musicality. In the early experimental piece "next year or i fly my rounds tempestuous," pasted into a 1934 appointment book offering a dose of biweekly good sense, small fragmentary poems are superimposed over the wholesome homilies: "If you circle / the habit of / your meaning, / it's fact and / no harm / done" and "Good deed, my / love. The ele- / ment of folk- / time. Nerves / are my past / monogamy, / said her arms / going farther. / Rock me out." The sequence bridges what Penberthy characterizes as Niedecker's surrealist period and her growing interest in aphoristic concision; and importantly, it is a graphic document of her elidings of plain speech and improvisational energies.

This preoccupation with wedding public possession to a fierce intimacy makes for fascinating tensions in Niedecker's work. *New Goose*, a project spanning 1935 to 1944, marks a conscious turn in crafting "folk poems," many full of scenes and voices of lives unraveled by the Depression. Often as brief as four or five lines, these poems offer quick, mordant glimpses of their figures' exhausted circumstances:

> Seven years a charming woman wore
> her coat, removed the collar where it tore,
> little warmth but honor in her loose
> thin coat, without knowing why
> she's so. Charming? Well, she's destitute.

Scarcity of means is made material in this poem's strict economy of sound: with the recurrence of "coat" and "charming," its mutually implicated terms, the scene circles to its acrid close on the one attention-grabbing word, "destitute," not only the lone three-syllable word, but a distanced and analytic label for the woman's poverty. The t sounds of "coat" and "destitute" crack sharply amidst the long open vowels and wash of m's and w's, with the poem's close a brusque break from the numbing circularity. The last word snaps reader, implicit viewer, and even the speaker from any seductive figure of ennobling poverty and complicates the central term of "honor." The poem becomes an honoring only when the woman's condition is named accurately, in its harshest term, as humiliation. The stumbles and reorientations of the last line, signaled by period, question mark, and comma, reveal the effort required to complete this contradictory act: stripping the "charming" qualifier, a garment of false dignity, to permit the ethical act of accurate seeing.

Throughout the *New Goose* poems, polyphony builds in a swift shifting of voice and scene, a commonality based on these spare tellings, but one that emphasizes separation and accretion, not concordance. Language becomes an outered excess available to all, the single shared possession, but muteness and invisibility are more powerful opposers and possessers. Circumscription governs these glancings into the inarticulate, with an awareness of borders and boundaries and the wide histories that lie beyond them, renewed at every line's turn: "Black Hawk held: In reason / land cannot be sold, / only things to be carried away, / and I am old."

Initially imagined as an updating of *Mother Goose* reflecting contemporary folk speech, Niedecker's project echoes that collection's eclecticism. The terse puzzling pieces that make up the nursery rhymes of Niedecker's model are believed to have been passed down orally over hundreds of years, often with little change, from sources as workaday as a street vendor's cry and as inflammatory as a war song. Mother Goose herself first appeared in France in 1697 as the fictional source of *Contes de ma mere l'Oye* and was co-opted and anglicized for *Mother Goose's Melody or Sonnets for the Cradle*, an assemblage of traditional rhymes appearing in England about 1765. The nursery rhymes every child knows extend back through histories few adults can imagine. Such uncertainty of authorship and ownership appealed to Niedecker, whose own avid appropriations and adaptations complicated the poet's role as sole proprieter and source. The book's "New" appellation is itself complicated by the poems' frequent drawing on historical documents; Niedecker worked as a researcher for the WPA, compiling materials for a Wisconsin guidebook. Her sense of place as presence finds expression in the sounds of colloquial speech, as well as in the traces of historical voices left in letters and oral histories: "Asa Gray wrote Increase Lapham: / pay particular attention / to my pets, the grasses."

While *New Goose* cedes aphoristic utterance to a series of shifting scenes and speakers, making wisdom a communal production, the poems of "for paul," written between 1949 and 1953, present a more unified though distanced speaker and a precise goal: the "further instruction" of a young child. The child in question was Louis Zukofsky's son, born in 1943, a violin prodigy of whom Niedecker was passionately fond. In 1931, Niedecker read the Objectivist issue of *Poetry* edited by Zukofsky,[3] a discovery she credited with the course of her later development. In writing to him, she initiated a thirty-five-year correspondence as well as a complex relationship; Niedecker's place in Paul's life was certainly complicated by her becoming pregnant by Zukofsky in 1933 and, at his insistence, aborting the child. The two poets maintained their friendship and a close exchange of work and mutual critique. Zukofsky sent Niedecker books and journals and assumed a role in the disposition of her work; he first referred her to Harriet Monroe at *Poetry* and promoted her early work and the *New Goose* poems to influential editors. But the poems of "for paul," some incorporating quotations from Zukofsky's letters or scenes of a not unconflicted family life, could draw his sharp and sometimes preemptory critique; it is questionable to what degree he may have been responsible for their scant publication. Even in the poems collaging quotes from letters and Niedecker's reading, a shadowy speaker is palpably present, assuming the role of a sibylline aunt instructing the boy in the complexities and powers inherent in "the three virtues / knowledge, humanity, energy." Much of the sequence concerns the legislation of such potencies; the figure of the young prodigy possessed of powers beyond his understanding or full ability to articulate and delimit is strangely conflated with an image of the childlike Einstein, whose questionable governance of his genius unleashes nightmare:

> Einstein, you know, said space
> is what it's made up of.
> And as to the human race
> "Why do you deeply oppose its passing"
> you'll find men asking
> the man with the nebular hair
>   and the fiddle.[4]

The sequence feels the child's private world as apart and essentially amoral: "he's been true to himself, a knife / behaved." Between the honoring of this privacy and the compulsion to offer guidance through a cultural geography of peril, possibility, and postwar vulnerabilty, a strange music forms. Niedecker is more than ever the shrewd aphorist—"Green, prickly humanity— / men are plants whose goodness grows / out of the soil, Mr. Stinkweed / or Mrs. Rose" and "Generator boy, Paul, love is carried / if it's held."—but at the same time, even more acutely tuned to musicality and nonsense sound: "Hi, Hot-and-Humid / That June she's a lush / Marshmushing, frog bickering / moon pooling, green gripping." In an inversion of hierarchy typical of Niedecker, the child becomes a diminutive muse authorizing rich dimensions of disciplined play:

> If he's not peewee wafted
>> tiny glissando
>> in deep shade
> or a newspaper
> he'll attack exercises ever calculated
> to float the ear in beauty.[5]

In this poem, a portrait of the artist as very young prodigy, we find a marvelously compressed catalogue of the contradictory forces in artistic making, laziness and distraction prominent among them; the making of music comes about only "if he's not" rapt in competing forms of action. Inseparable from his sensory world, the child is expressed as pure music and movement: lines 2 and 3 sound a rapid run of shifting long and short vowels, while "wafted" and the rippling "glissando" lighten into motion—then the abrupt rhythmic counterpoint of line 4's heavily stressed monosyllables momentarily suspends the poem before the comic deflationary dailiness of "a newspaper." Temptations lurk at all levels of diction. The final lines echo and vary this opposition of rhythm and sound; the child's discipline and fierce focus are felt in the sharp syllables of "attack," "ex," and "calc," mental actions far from the dreamy wafting a few lines before, but the attack's aim is the sonorous "to float the ear"; it is the cerebral abstractions of calculated exercises that allow the listener's sensual connection, that in effect make the listener a listening, entirely ear. Economies of pleasure, with the completion of the artistic act not simply a mediation of spontaneity and design, but a transaction of energies that finds completion in engaging the audience in the dynamic relational network. Music as a mode of thought recurs in this frail pastoral:

Paul
    when the leaves
        fall

from their stems
    that lie thick
        on the walk

in the light
    of the full note
        the moon
playing
    to leaves
        when they leave

the little
    thin things
        Paul[6]

What constitutes knowledge? A sound, a glinting quickness, a branching of relations. In a later poem, Niedecker adapts a famous quote from Hopkins's journals, his search for "the law of the oak leaves."[7] The leaves' law is an intricacy of pattern, a material intelligence articulating its relational interdependencies; in this poem, as eminently in Hopkins, sound pattern makes the poem a material analogue to natural profusion and its ceaseless self-expression. Relations of sound leap across divisions of line and syntax, multiplying pattern and annulling hierarchical subordination. As pastoral, it enacts a radical merging of nature mediated in language and language assuming the material complexity of an organic form: the poem as a mobile, thinking body. For the child prodigy whose intuitive grasp of pattern outpaces his power to extend these relational acts, instruction resides in a modeling of that motion; the moon's note is the resonant music linking leaf-strewn walk and lunar orbit and is the round radiating sonic center of the poem's torque.

Niedecker's later writings found themselves more broadly on the shared spaces of nature and history. Folk poem and "for paul"'s looser movements give way to haiku-like tautness. The haiku tradition and its presumed objectivity would have appealed to her, as would its sometimes overt questioning of that distance. Many haiku contain a turn toward the personal, a sometimes comic rupturing of the illusion of non-mediation revealing the observer-transcriber's investment and implication in the moment's assembling. Issa's "Fleas in my hut / it's my fault / you look so skinny" (in Robert Hass's version)[8] places man democratically in the ecosystem and teases the implicit hierarchy of the food chain. "Plainness and oddness are the bones of haikai," wrote Basho, a formulation Niedecker could not not have loved. In her adaptation of the form, haiku's compression and swiftness are married to her sound-play:

> Lights, lifts
> parts nicely opposed
> this white
>   lice lithe
> pink bird[9]

In another instance, "People, people— / ten dead duck's feathers / on beer can litter . . . / Winter / will change all that,"[10] the subtle malevolence of the speaker afflicted by marauding tourists gives the haiku convention of seasonal flux a palpably personal and local application.

Such extreme compression carries over into the final collections, where terse fragments gain resonance by their contiguities within longer sequences. Always concerned with place and how it permeates, Niedecker in *North Central* (1968) maps a geological genealogy, "a lovely / finite parentage / mineral / vegetable / animal" linking the human to the greater complex: "A man / bends to inspect / a shell / Himself / part coral / and mud / clam."[11] Acutely aware of the material, the sequence sometimes abandons syntax for meticulous catalogues of substances, textures, and sinuous names, from the rocky presences of the opening sections—"Ruby of corundum / lapis lazuli / from changing limestone / glow-apricot red-brown / carnelian sard"—to the sly, profligate flora of "wintergreen ridge": "laurel in muskeg / Linnaeus' twinflower / Andromeda / Cisandra of the bog / pearl-flowered / Lady's tresses / insect-eating / pitcher plant / Bedeviled little Drosera / of the sundews / deadly / in spaghum moss." In this longer poem, with its winding associational movement, Niedecker is the poet of profuse and riotous nature,

one not excluding politics as local as a don't-pick-the-flowers sign
and as global as the Bomb. Here nature calls the poet to a consciousness of larger relational systems, a reminder of multiplicity
and mutual implication, but as always with Niedecker an awareness of delineation and limit.

Like the sequences of *North Central*, the strongly autobiographical "paean to place" employs a longer associative structure, here
in five-line stanzas. "Place" serves as a meditative ground encom-
passing geographical rooting, class, circumstance—the social conditions of family—and even artistic vocation as interwoven placings
that determine the speaker's trajectory and range of imaginative
motion. In contrast, *Harpsichord & Salt Fish*, the last manuscript Niedecker completed before her death in 1970, subsumes authorial
presence almost completely; its central poems assume the voices
of historical personae—Jefferson, Darwin, William Morris—visionary precisionists caught in contradiction. In her essay on the first
twelve sections of Zukofsky's A, Niedecker describes his model of
Shakespeare as "a chart of learning to be taken lightly," and her
own sense of the learned and received seems a process of brush-
ings and slight shadings and sensations. Her personae assume
presence in their relations to ephemera, the momentary flashing
out and releasing of the historical figure from his flat continuum,
disrupting the false coherence imposed by time and distance.
Sensory immediacy bridges and breaks in, often captured in the
speech cadences of letters quoted or adapted:

> Political honors
>   "splendid torments"
> "If one could establish
>   an absolute power
> of silence over oneself"
>
> When I set out for Monticello
>   (my grandchildren
> will they know me?)
> How are my young
> chestnut trees?
> ("THOMAS JEFFERSON")

These lines are concerned not least with different possibilities for scoring voice, the range of modulations possible in quotation marks, parentheses, question marks, the launching into motion of a "when" or "how." Jefferson's concern with frost on the strawberries, Darwin "ravenous / for the sound / of the pianoforte"[12]: these luminous instants take their place in the reader's imaginative structuring of a historical consciousness—in this case, of builders of elegant structures—and in the formal structuring of a poem. The phrase "harpsichord and salt fish" is nearly a poem in itself, a type of the kinetic contiguity at which Niedecker excelled, launching a range of opposing textures, motions, and systems: the musical and mute, the metallic and fleshy, instrument and product, drawing room and dock, sound and taste, leisure and commerce, dactyl and spondee.

Penberthy's edition aims to replace the 1985 *From This Condensery: The Complete Writing of Lorine Niedecker*, which she disparages for rampant inaccuracies, and to provide a complement and counterpoint to two different volumes of *Collected Poems* (T&G, prepared in 1965 and published in 1969, and the 1970 *My Life by Water*), for which Niedecker arranged her work in categories such as "Home / World" and "In Exchange for Haiku." Penberthy presents instead a chronological arrangement, restoring the dismantled manuscripts of projected books and ordering the uncollected work often falling between projects, but observing Niedecker's final revisions to individual poems as prepared for *My Life by Water*. This is a bewildering history, which Penberthy takes care to clarify by providing contents pages for the previous volumes and cross-references to the poem's prior groupings. Her meticulous notes on revisions are intriguing reading and at times take on their subject's voice— "The spelling of 'Einsteind' is consistent in all appearances" has an unmistakable Niedeckerean deadpan. In her zeal to replace a Niedecker appreciated largely for her folk poems with a language-centered poet whose early experiments are crucial to her exploit, Penberthy at times employs the expectable excess of a revisionist reading. But her extraordinary efforts to bring to light Niedecker's importance are utterly invaluable, including editorship of the correspondence with Zukofsky, the unearthing of early poems, and the sustained archival scrutiny leading to this sadly belated—and, as she notes, still partial and speculative—realization of the poet's intents.

Among poets, the appearance of this volume, and the recent selected poems of Rae Armantrout and Fanny Howe, may point to a curious, circuitous winding of a subtle minimalist tradition, Dickinsonian slantness tensed in spare speech. With its range of tonalities and mobilities, Niedecker's work explodes the standard cliches of minimalism as quiet or modest. The poet who ends an elegy rejecting "Heaven? / No, restore / my matter, never free from motion / to the soil's roar" is not quiet or modest, but an expansive, essential intelligence who must be read.

...NOTES...

1. [Lorine Niedecker, "Traces of Living Things," in *Collected Works*, edited by Jenny Penberthy (Berkeley: University of California Press, 2002), p. 240.]

2. [See *Poetry: A Magazine of Verse* 42:6 (September 1933): pp. 308–309.

3. [See *Poetry: A Magazine of Verse* 37:5 (February 1931): pp. 237–296. Besides Zukofsky's "Program: 'Objectivists' 1931," this issue includes pieces by Carl Rakosi, Charles Reznikoff, Kenneth Rexroth, George A. Oppen, Basil Bunting, and William Carlos Williams.]

4. [Niedecker, *Collected Works*, pp. 139–140.]

5. [Ibid., p. 147.]

6. [Ibid., p. 156.]

7. [See Hopkins's journal entry for 19 July 1866: *The Journals and Papers of Gerard Manley Hopkins*, edited by Humphry House, completed by Graham Storey (London: Oxford University Press, 1959), p. 146.]

8. [*The Essential Haiku: Versions of Basho, Buson, and Issa*, edited and with verse translations by Robert Hass (Hopewell, N.J.: Ecco, 1994): p. 174.]

9. [Niedecker, *Collected Works*, p. 218.]

10. ["Wintergreen Ridge," ibid., p. 252.]

11. ["Traces of Living Things," ibid., p. 239.]

12. ["Darwin," ibid., p. 296.]

...PERMISSIONS...

...CONTRIBUTORS...

Stephen Burt teaches at Macalester College in St. Paul, Minnesota. His books include two collections of poetry, *Parallel Play* (2006) and *Popular Music* (1999); a critical study, *Randall Jarrell and His Age* (2002); and a scholarly edition, *Randall Jarrell on W. H. Auden* (2005). His website is www.accommodatingly.com.

Jorie Graham was born and grew up in Rome. Her books of poems include *The Dream of the Unified Field* (1995), which won the Pulitzer Prize, *The Errancy* (1998), *Swarm* (2001), and *Overlord* (2005), all from Ecco. The recipient of many fellowships and awards, she is the Boylston Professor of Rhetoric and Oratory at Harvard University.

James Harms is the author of four books of poetry: *Freeways and Aqueducts* (2004), *Quarters* (2001), *The Joy Addict* (1998), and *Modern Ocean* (1992). His awards include fellowships from the National Endowment for the Arts, the PEN/Revson Foundation, the Pennsylvania and West Virginia Arts Commissions, Bread Loaf, and the MacDowell Colony. He directs the MFA Program in Creative Writing at West Virginia University.

Lyn Hejinian's most recently published books include *A Border Comedy, My Life in the Nineties*, and *The Fatalist*. *The Language of Inquiry*, a collection of essays, was published in 2000. She is the co-director, with Travis Ortiz, of *Atelos*, a literary project commissioning and publishing cross-genre work by poets. She teaches in the English Department of the University of California, Berkeley.

Mark Jarman is the author of *Body and Soul: Essays on Poetry* and *To the Green Man*, a collection of poetry. He teaches at Vanderbilt University.

Donald Justice won the Pulitzer Prize for his *Selected Poems* (1979). He was the co-winner of the 1991 Bollingen Prize. In 1992 he was elected to the American Academy and Institute of Arts and Letters. Throughout his career he taught at various universities, including long stints at both the University of Iowa's Writers' Workshop and the University of Florida. He died on 6 August 2004, shortly before the publication of his *Collected Poems*.

Dennis O'Driscoll was born in Thurles, County Tipperary. His seven books of poetry include *Weather Permitting* (1999), *Exemplary Damages* (2002), and *New & Selected Poems* (2004). A selection of his essays and reviews, *Troubled Thoughts, Majestic Dreams*, was published in 2001. He received the Lannan Literary Award in 1999 and the 2005 E. M. Forster Award of the American Academy of Arts and Letters. He has worked as a civil servant in Dublin since the age of sixteen.

Helen Vendler has published studies of such figures as Shakespeare, Herbert, Keats, and Stevens. Her many titles include *Part of Nature, Part of Us: Modern American Poets* (1980), *The Music of What Happens: Poems, Poets, Critics* (1988), *The Breaking of Style: Hopkins, Heaney, Graham* (1995), and *Poets Thinking: Pope, Whitman, Dickinson, Yeats* (2004). Her writing appears regularly in the *New Republic* and the *London Review of Books*. She is the A. Kingsley Porter University Professor at Harvard University.

Karen Volkman is the author of *Crash's Law* (1996) and *Spar* (2002), which received the Iowa Poetry Prize and the 2002 James Laughlin Award from the Academy of American Poets. Her poems have appeared in *The Pushcart Prize Anthology*, *Best American Poetry*, and *Twenty-first Century Poetics*. Recipient of fellowships and awards from the National Endowment for the Arts, the Poetry Society of America, and the Akademie Schloss Solitude, she teaches on the MFA faculty at the University of Montana.

Joshua Weiner is the author of *The World's Room*, a book of poems. His criticism appears in a variety of journals. He is the recipient of a Whiting Writer's Award, the Witter Bynner Fellowship at the Library of Congress, and the Joseph Brodsky Rowe Prize in Literature from the American Academy of Arts and Letters. He is assistant professor of English at the University of Maryland, College Park.

Stephen Yenser's books of poems are *Blue Guide* (2006) and *The Fire in All Things* (2002), which won the Walt Whitman Award from the Academy of American Poets. Among his critical works are *Circle to Circle: The Poetry of Robert Lowell* (1975), *The Consuming Myth: The Work of James Merrill* (1987), and *A Boundless Field: American Poetry at the Century's Turning* (2002). With J. D. McClatchy, he is editing James Merrill's collected works, the fourth and most recent volume of which is *The Charging Light at Sandover* (2006).

...INDEX...